BARBED
+ THORNS

BARBED WIRE + THORNS

A Christian's Reflection on Suffering

LENA MALMGREN

Translated by Richard J. Erickson

HENDRICKSON PUBLISHERS

Barbed Wire and Thorns: A Christian's Reflection on Suffering
English translation © 2007 by Hendrickson Publishers, Inc.
P. O. Box 3473
Peabody, Massachusetts 01961-3473

ISBN 978-1-59856-044-2

Translated from *Taggtråd och törne: Texter för fasten och andra tider då tröst behövs.*
Lund: Arcus, 2002.

The poems written by Joyce Tenghamm that introduce each section were translated from the Swedish and used with permission.

Printed in the United States of America

First Printing — July 2007

Library of Congress Cataloging-in-Publication Data

Malmgren, Lena.
  [Taggtråd och törne. English]
  Barbed wire and thorns : a Christian's reflection on suffering /
Lena Malmgren ; translated by Richard J. Erickson.
    p. cm.
  Includes bibliographical references.
  ISBN 978-1-59856-044-2 (alk. paper)
  1. Jesus Christ—Passion. 2. Suffering—Religious aspects—
Christianity. 3. Suffering—Biblical teaching. I. Title.
  BT431.3.M3613 2007
  248.8′6—dc22
                                2007013991

For Maia

Table of Contents

Introduction

I've written about Easter and the Resurrection before, and I will yet again. This, however, is a book both for Lent and for every other time[1] when consolation is needed or when questions arise about suffering and about the meaning of life. I have written now about Jesus and his struggle to fulfill his calling, especially in his last days. In the meditations around Jesus' death I have sought to understand more what it was like for him than what we might think it means for us. These little essays can be read straight through in order, if the reader wishes, but there is actually no strict sequence to the book. Or one may dip into it here and there at will.

I have also written on questions about temptation and the struggle against evil, about illness and other forms of suffering, about the bread of life and atonement. The perspective is my own. I am a woman and a pastor, and for many years now I have been afflicted with a condition known as fibromyalgia, which causes me much pain and fatigue.

I make use of the Synoptic Gospels mostly, but I've also used texts about Thomas from the Gospel of John, as well as others. Where the same material exists in more than one of the Synoptics, I have chiefly followed Mark, since it is the earliest of the three and since Matthew and Luke both have access to Mark as they write.

With the church and most scholarship, I have followed John's chronology. I assume along with John that Jesus' active ministry was spread over a period of three Passovers, that is to say, a period of two or three years. The parallel between John 6 and Matthew 14 places the latter story at the second of these three Passovers, when Jesus was not in Jerusalem. I also assume with John that Jesus died on the day before the Jewish Passover.

There is no general agreement on the exact chronological order of the many recorded events in Jesus' life. Even the Passion Narrative is given with some variations among the four Gospels. The other Gospel materials are assembled according each evangelist's own thematic method—each of them without a doubt carefully considered, though more or less inscrutable to us. As a framework for the period of Jesus' life that focuses on his passion—namely, from the day he determined to set out for Jerusalem to the day of his crucifixion—I have chosen Luke's Travel Narrative in chapters 9–19. Luke (9:51–56) doesn't mention the place where Jesus began his final journey, but the parallels in Mark (10:1; cf. 9:33) and Matthew (19:1–2) suggest it was his home territory, in both cases Capernaum, to which he and his followers had recently returned after spending some time in the region of Caesarea Philippi (Mark 8:27; Matthew 16:13).

Otherwise, the passages I cite or allude to are often chosen from the Lenten texts recommended in *Den Svenska Evangeliehandboken 2002*. For the English translation, these texts are usually cited according to the New Revised Standard Version of the Bible. Sometimes I quote a biblical text rather freely and sometimes I retell a story in my own words. Likewise, I vary my style according to the character of the texts, from the everyday, to the purely objective, to the poetical. I have been inspired in these freer renderings through Danish translations done by Anna Sophie Seidelin and Paul Seidelin as well as through the Jerusalem Bible.

At the end of nearly every meditation, for reference and for the readers' convenience, I have listed the biblical texts on which I have based my thoughts. Readers should feel free, indeed encouraged, to look up these texts and compare them with what I have written. The various biblical passages could certainly be used as texts for daily devotions, even though I have not included them with this purpose in mind.

Both the English and Greek languages have vocabulary words that refer either to a specific gender—*girl* for example—or to both genders, such as *sibling*. They also have words that can function both ways, either referring to a single gender *or* to both genders; we sometimes call these terms "inclusive" words. The English word *dog* belongs in this latter category. Consider the following: "Do you have a dog or a cat?"—"I have a dog."—"Is it a dog or a bitch?"—"It's a dog." An especially sensitive Greek word in this regard is *adelphoi*, which can mean either "brothers," or siblings of both sexes. I translate the word with *siblings* or *brothers and sisters* wherever it is not obviously wrong to do so. In applying this method to texts from Mark's Gospel, I have benefited directly from Fredrik Ivarsson's inclusive translation in his "The Gospel according to Mark and Mary" (*Tro & Tanke*, 1999:4); elsewhere I follow his model.

Since deity does not have gender, I have tried to avoid referring to God as either "he" or "she," unless I am quoting another source, a confirmation student, for example. Whenever I use the word "Lord," I have in mind Jesus Christ, whom I regard without reservation as my Lord.

The word *disciples* has various senses in the New Testament. Sometimes it stands for "the Twelve," the circle of twelve men Jesus gathered around himself. Sometimes it refers to a larger circle of disciples that included women (cf. Luke 8:1–3; 9:1–2; 10:1). The number of those who traveled with him varied from time to time as people joined themselves to his band (Luke 9:57) or left him (John 6:66). The word *apostle* is sometimes used as a synonym for one of "the Twelve," but in Acts 1:26 Matthias was chosen as an apostle to succeed Judas Iscariot. Paul and Barnabas are also designated as apostles, not just Paul alone (e.g., Acts 14:14); likewise Andronicus and Junia in Romans 16:7.

I have read hundreds of books, both religious and profane, on the subjects of suffering, evil, grief and crisis, and death, and I am not counting those belonging to the more literary genres. Three in particular have helped me both in living and in thinking: Ludvig

Jönsson, *Uppgörelse med allmakten och döden* [Reconciling Omnipotence and Death], Harold Kushner, *When Bad Things Happen to Good People,* and Nathan Söderblom, *Humor och melankoli och andra lutherstudier* [Humor and Melancholy, and Other Studies in Luther]. I have also returned to Luther's thoughts on *Deus absconditus* (The Hidden God), which I wrote about for Gustaf Wingren[2] in 1974 and which became an essential element in my faith perspective.

The discussion groups on Christian faith that gathered at my home for years have given shape to many of the questions that surface in this book—and that find some sort of answers there. In the same way, groups who have practiced preaching together with me in the Pastoral Institute in Lund have given me ideas and inspiration. I thank you all!

Names of the persons who appear in the texts have been changed for the most part, in order to protect their privacy. The Anna in the meditation "A Woman and a Half" actually has a different name. Charlott and Ninni, who are identified with their own forenames, have given me permission for that, as has Inga-Lill's husband. Again, my thanks.

My husband, Professor Birger Olsson, has checked my use of Scripture and answered a thousand questions. In no way, however, is he responsible for my conclusions. Thank you, Birger! Thanks as well to all others who know they have supported me either by reading texts or by bearing me up, body and soul, in some other way, especially my physical therapist, Marie Louise Fredborn. Thanks to Pastor Anna Eklund, agronomist Fredrik Stendahl, and my co-minister Joyce Tenghamn, for reading the entire manuscript in various stages. I particularly wish to single out Joyce, who shares with me the experience of pain and who wanted to share with me in this book as well. The poems introducing each section of the book are written by her. Other poems are mine, unless I have indicated differently.

Through Darkness into Light

Why me, Lord?
Just when life
had opened to
its bright pages.

Why not me?
Now the Word
can inscribe its light
even on my dark leaves.

The Answer, If There Is One
(Isa 60:19; Matt 10:39)

To Go or Not to Go

Matt 10:25; Jer 9:23–24; Phil 1:3–11, 3:7–14

February has begun, a short month that always feels long. It is cold, damp and gray—gray, gray, gray, with glistening black on the naked trunks and branches of the trees. They look dead, but they have merely withdrawn their strength deep down into their roots. They have already put forth new buds. Imagine, if I were only like a tree, I could blame my lack of strength on new buds.

It has taken a long time to come to this point, to the point of writing about suffering. To be honest I know why, of course. It has to do not just with illness and all the demands of daily life that we place on ourselves and on each other, and with the little time and strength we have left over. It has to do with utter exhaustion.

A traditional hymn invites us as disciples of Jesus: "Behold, we go up to Jerusalem."[3] I sing along, but I am reluctant, too—do I even want to think about this matter of suffering one more time? Am I afraid of suffering? Yes, I clearly am, and it would be perverse of me not to fear it. I don't want any more of it, thank you very much, at least not if I have a choice about it. I don't want any more of it in my own life, nor in anyone else's either. I am so weary of the whole thing. Just thinking and writing about suffering is like digging a well in hard ground; it is not some mere fluttering of wings. It creates a kind of defenselessness within me, against both unkindness and interruptions; I can feel it as soon as I begin.

On the other hand, I can easily imagine myself going up to Jerusalem among Jesus' disciples during his final weeks, perhaps as one of the women who followed him from Galilee. I am glad to do it. I love him just as they did, and his actions at the end of his life have a special sort of consistency that attracts me.

Yet this journey he makes, God's struggle against evil, ends in powerlessness. Of course, it doesn't actually *end* that way, but it does for all practical purposes, since its true end—his victory—is for now so colossally out there, "beyond" the here and now. His victory cannot come until after he endures the powerlessness of life and the victory of death.

It should be enough for a disciple if she endures what her Master endures. Naturally! The comfort in this duty is both the knowledge that every evil thing will one day be abolished, and the certainty that the Master is always near. But that comfort comes with no promise that powerlessness and lack of strength will loosen their grip on us during our time here on earth.

I am not saying that I like it this way! Luther's advice doesn't come easy for me, to fix my eyes on the devil and roar at him, to scream into the darkness at the eyes watching me there (if there really are eyes watching me at all): "Just remember, Satan! You are more transient than I am!"

"Certainty"—is that the right word for his nearness? Well, perhaps. "Perception" isn't right; it's too much a sense-based word, and rarely are the senses involved in an encounter with God, as in touching the hem of a garment or in feeling the caress of a wing. Yet his nearness is more than just saying, "I feel his presence"—something that happens far less often than *always*, in any case. It probably doesn't matter so much; truly enduring and resilient love, the sort one has for one's family, is not something that one always feels either. I can be as irritated as I like with those nearest to me or so utterly overcome with weariness that I feel nothing at all, yet I know that I love them just the same. And faith is most like that kind of love.

"Yes, but how does it feel" asked one of the students in my confirmation class. "What does it feel like to have real contact with God when you pray?"

"Well," I tried to answer, "at its best, it's brightness and warmth and closeness, like being screened off from everything else."

"Ah," he replied. "Like living inside the same light bulb with God."

Maybe so. Almost everything that has to do with God has to be described in pictures, many pictures, even contradictory or paradoxical pictures. Having God nearby is also like riding the trolley when I was a schoolgirl in Gothenburg. A pole stood in the middle of the open platforms at either end of the trolley, and we had to hang on to it as the car swung and lurched. The God of all the ages is like that pole.

Or it's like finally seeing my most dearly beloved again, like a closeness to which even my skin presents no barrier and in which to touch each other is to join together what was meant to be a unity. It is as when we look into each other's eyes and rest in one another, as when we see and recognize and love each other, as when even my very skull seems transparent and time turns inside out, and wings dance in the mist above a waterfall.

I look at Sunday's text from Jeremiah; he speaks grimly as usual. Well he might, for he was a man of much affliction. "Thus says the Lord: Do not let the wise boast in their wisdom, do not let the mighty boast in their might, do not let the wealthy boast in their wealth."

Borrowing an expression of my grandchild, I reply, "Okay, prophet! I won't boast, even though sometimes I feel as if I were a thousand years old and had seen everything there is to see and had tasted enough of life to be wise forever. Can't I take some pride in having learned a little along the way? Shouldn't I perhaps be able to find a little more strength to ponder over?" (And I'm just talking about physical strength, in my muscles, rather than about some sort of inner quality.) As for riches, I'm not likely ever to become wealthy, and that's a relief of sorts, just as it is also a relief to have the means to buy new shoes when the old ones fall apart.

Jeremiah goes on: "But let those who boast, boast in this, that they understand and know me, that I am the Lord; I act with stead-fast love."

Here now we definitely have something. When the Lord God resolves a matter, he does not do it through human wisdom or strength or riches—or through power, for that matter. He has only one method of operating: through love.

But what is that supposed to mean? What does it look like? How am I supposed to understand it? Still worse, Paul says in his letter to the Philippians that even my judgments about things— perhaps my entire intellect?—must follow in the path of love. "And this is my prayer, that your love may overflow more and more with knowledge and full insight to help you to determine what is best."

There is no doubt that I must go to Jerusalem. I read further in Philippians: "I want to know Christ and the power of his resurrection and the sharing of his sufferings."

Seed on Bare Rock

Luke 8:4–15; Ps 33:4–9

It's mid-February, and I'm driving home in the evening. Actually it's only the afternoon, but the asphalt is black and the darkness of the northern winter obscures both sides of the road. Off in the distance the lights of the city of Malmö color the horizon with a sulfur-yellow glow. The almanac insists that the day has lengthened by twenty minutes at both ends, but one can scarcely tell. Most people still commute to and from work in the dark.

This morning I was in too much pain to go to the church, but I am familiar with the Gospel text for this week. A man went out to sow—and he went about it rather strangely. He wasted the seed by sowing it in various kinds of unsuitable and unfruitful ground. What kind of harvest was he hoping to get among thistles or out of a thin layer of soil covering the bedrock? How could he have entertained such a hope?

If he were Jesus, he would have entertained exactly such a hope. Jesus sowed in all possible and impossible places, and he hoped for a harvest among all possible and impossible people. Some of the seed fell on bare rock. Sometimes I'm part of the circle of his followers who constitute that bare rock, and this seed is one thing we have in common. The seed that actually falls on unfruitful ground, so hopeless there that the merest breeze carries it away, is his thrice-repeated word: "The Son of Man must suffer and die." It doesn't sink in. We don't want to receive it. The others don't and neither do I.

Not suffering and death, no more of that; I am so unbelievably tired of it, just as tired of it as I am of winter darkness, and of slush and of the icy wind on my neck.

Yet these are questions we can't let go of. Everyone asks them. Why does suffering exist? If there is a God, why does the world look like this? Why do the innocent die? Where does evil come from? Why should it even exist at all?

Or closer to home: Why *me?* What have *I* done to deserve this?

There are no clear answers to such questions. Not even in the Bible. I certainly am not able to give much of an answer. At best, we can only offer one another mere scraps of the truth, or we can point in a certain direction and say, "Go there, or think about it this way; it's what I did, and it helped me a little."

But I am absolutely certain of at least one thing. If we are ever to find Christian answers to questions about the meaning of suffering, we will have to look for them in what Christ himself did, and presumably most of all in the story of his own suffering. We could obviously concoct an answer that gives us a picture of God different from the picture Jesus gives us, but we could not call it a Christian answer. A portrait of God that does not reflect the face of Christ as he approached Golgotha would not be a portrait of *our* God.

We seek God and the answers to our questions by turning our face to the stars. But we won't find God there. More likely we'll find God lying in the gutter. We want a strong hand to guide us and to keep us from danger as we make our way in the world. But *God's* hand bears the wounds of nails and the marks of powerlessness. We look for God in logic and philosophy. But the identity of the power that sustains the earth, of the one who brought forth the skies and space by a word, of the one who gathered the sea in a bottle and put the waters of the deep in a storehouse—the identity of *this* power is love.

At times it can be downright irritating, this need to describe God in mere pictures. It is easy to wish we had something less ambiguous. But it isn't any different from the way we think about ourselves. I cannot define myself. As soon as I try to get a grip on who I am exactly, I end up with, well, just pictures. I speak of situations in which I sense or know that I acted in a way typical for me, or even peculiar to just me. I riffle through pictures in my mind in order somehow to capture exactly who I am. That is about as close as I can come.

We cannot get any closer to God than this either. We want to define God according to our own conceptions and thinking, and in line with our own desire to live our lives in our own way. We want to draw God on graph paper. But if we think that we have captured or defined God, then it is something other than God we have captured. God will not be ensnared, neither by our words and formulas nor by our desires. But God does come to us in a suffering and struggling person, and we may, with hope, look there.

Going up to Jerusalem

Thank you, blessed God,
that I find
no meaning
in what is meaningless.
This is precisely why
I endure.

What Is Meaningful

Here Begins the Great Loneliness

Luke 18:31–34; Luke 10:1; Acts 1:15; Joel 2:28–29, cf. Acts 2:17–18;
Luke 9:51; Luke 8:1–3; Mark 1:9; Mark 1:14; Mark 6, cf. Matt 14; John 3:30

He has made up his mind, this Jesus from Nazareth. He will go up to Jerusalem for the Passover. He has already talked about it before, explaining that he will be conveyed there into the custody of the people, that both pagans and devout Jews will do with him as they please. For now, however, his friends have only a dim idea of what he is about to do. Nor dare they ask him more. They probably suspect that he won't tell them what they would like to know anyway.

This, clearly, is how the great loneliness begins. Otherwise, the situation is difficult to grasp, very difficult. Why do I think so? There are many people around him; that is also clear. Exactly how many, we can only guess, but shortly after his departure he is able to select seventy-two disciples for a preaching tour. Later, when the congregation gathers in Jerusalem in the days following Easter, there are 120 persons—and that was before the Holy Spirit gave them courage to share publicly what had happened to them.

This means it is time to lay aside the image that I for one so long envisioned, a picture of twelve men accompanying him quietly and with dignity up to the temple. Instead, the circumstances surrounding him were surely very messy and intense. What a time it must have been just to get underway every morning! Somehow or another, people needed food in their stomachs, and no doubt problems arose, somewhere, whenever they broke camp.

There were lots of people with him then, both women and men, poor and rich, old and young, exactly as it was at Pentecost, just as the prophet Joel predicted; Luke quotes him here: "Your sons and your daughters shall prophesy, and your young men shall see visions, and your old men shall dream dreams. Even upon my slaves, both men and women, in those days I will pour out my Spirit." Some of these folks were from the lower middle class, like Jesus himself, with jobs, homes and families; others had lived as beggars and with constant sickness, or as poor wretches exploited in the sex trade.

In the midst of this crowd he is alone—and any one of us knows how *that* feels.

They were in his native territory, in the vicinity of Capernaum, Bethsaida, and the Sea of Galilee. Many of them came from these districts and probably took the opportunity to visit their families. Mary, one of the women who used her own assets for helping him, left perhaps to look after her business affairs or her sizable inheritance or whatever else she had in Magdala. Johanna, another of these women, may instead have been wary of going to Tiberias and the court of Herod Antipas—a man both weak and cruel, which is a very dangerous mixture.

I also suspect that Jesus himself went home to Nazareth. Apparently, his mother and a few of his siblings had agreed to accompany him this time, as had the mother of James and John. I visualize him going out into the workshop, where he had labored hard for so many years and where he had waited for the day when he would first set out on his calling. I think he stood there with Joseph's tools, turning them over in his hands, a plane, a knife, a wooden square.

Here is something I have learned through very difficult times. Objects are nothing other than what they appear to be. Objects, unlike human beings, are exactly what they are. They are good, innocent. A cat is entirely without guilt when it brings us a sparrow in its mouth. A horse that kicks the blacksmith who shoes it, a fire that warms a pot of oatmeal or burns a forest—they are guiltless. Similarly a loom, a plane, or a wooden spoon, all guiltless. There was a time when I thought there was something more, as if there were an inherent sensitivity, a pliability, a tenderness within a tool that made it look forward to my coming, as if it anticipated with joy the cheerful satisfaction of collaborating with a human being.

This is why I think he went home, to say goodbye to all his tools. Maybe there were some handmade spikes that he rolled around in his hand. Perhaps he lifted up a newly hewn beam that James had recently brought in, weighing it in his hands, and perhaps he saw the resin still running like tears along the grain of the wood. But soon both nail and beam would betray him.

I am tired, so tired. I can't even think straight. I lie down on the bed, working my aching back into a comfortable position, and begin to drift into sleep. Suddenly, I have it! John the Baptist! We call him the Forerunner, the one who prepares the way for Jesus. And rightly so. But this does not mean merely that he called people out to the Jordan and baptized the contrite until Jesus took over.

Jesus came from Nazareth in Galilee and was baptized by John in the Jordan. John was already baptizing before Jesus set out on his mission. When John was imprisoned, Jesus came to Galilee and proclaimed the gospel of God. When Jesus got the word about John's death, he began to tell his disciples who he himself was and about his own suffering and death.

Till now he had had his older cousin there, like a big brother, the one who had gone before him preparing the way, the one who had been great enough himself to recognize who was greater, and to realize that this was exactly as it should be. I also wondered whether John, who feared no one, could have kept silent even in the realm of the dead, where dragons guard the gates. He likely stood there and cried out to them, too: "You brood of vipers! Lift up these gates! Open wide these doors! You'd better be careful! For God is coming soon!"

But John is no longer there. Jesus has to make this decision on his own: to Jerusalem for the Passover this year or not? In one way, there is nothing wrong with this sort of thing. A decision made in solitude can be more authentic, more likely to come from within, provided one dares to get close enough to one's inner self. Although, for my part, I have no idea whether it would be easier or more difficult to do this in the face of death.

However it may be, now the great loneliness begins.

Pious Lies

Eph 1:9; Eph 2:10; 1 Tim 2:4–6; 2 Sam 18:19–33

There are plenty of pious lies. The ugliest of them I know is probably this one:

"Everything that happens has a meaning."

Meaning can be difficult to distinguish in the midst of everyday life, when sorrow and joy travel together, tightly interlaced. While I walk, literally, in the sunshine and summer breeze, a friend fights for his life following an operation. Television news is full of politicians who take bribes, or of a nuclear power plant gone defunct, or of another war somewhere—I should look it up in an atlas! Can we see a pattern here?

The pattern I see is one of struggle, between good and evil, between God and Satan. This is why it is difficult to discern meaning. It is also why meaningless things occur—a child is raped, a car skids out of control, a river overflows its banks. Chaos, emptiness, apathy, and sheer chance also make up the face of evil. The power that seeks above all to destroy naturally also exerts its influence against whatever gives stability and coherence to human existence—order, content, joy of life, and meaning.

But what about the ageless human question: "Is there any meaning *at all* in life?" I believe this question actually consists of two questions, perhaps several. The first of them is this: "Is there a God who has any sort of plan for the world, and do I have any place in that plan?"

Christian faith answers this with an unqualified yes. God lives and God has a plan for the world, to rescue it through Jesus Christ. God has created us for eternity as well, and does not wish us to stray from the road that leads us there. God also has a plan for our life here and now, on the earth. "Plan" in the language of the New Testament is the word *oikonomia*, the same word as our "economy." We could also translate it as "budget." We serve as resources in God's budget for the world. God enters our goodness toward each other on the income side of the ledger.

Some people have remarkable, special tasks given them by God, magnificent and heroic deeds. For most of us, however, our days fall into a myriad of small pieces, into a series of simple duties, and therefore they do not shine anywhere near so brightly. Yet our tasks are equally necessary. God uses them to build the world, working together with us. Together we heal and sooth, forgive and create, and create anew.

Still, God's plan is often sabotaged, both by us and by evil powers from outside. If God did not enter our goodness into the income column, there would be utter chaos. Of course, that lack of goodness isn't the entire explanation of the world's chaos, but it plays its part. Fortunately, God is quite good at improvising and at creating new plans based on new assumptions. It happens all the time.

Other people answer "no" to this first question about whether there is a god or a plan for the world. There is no god, either in life or in death, so far as human reason can say. No one is guiding the course of events toward a certain goal. No one cares what happens, for good or ill. We are at the mercy of blind chance. Or they may say, fatalistically, Time and Chance control everything.

The second question is one that everyone asks: "Is life worth living? Is it worth the trouble? Or do the difficult things of life—pain, loneliness, emptiness—outweigh its value, so that the most sensible thing would be simply to put an end to it?" Whether we believe in God or not, we bear a heavy responsibility for how we answer this question. We must do something worthwhile, something important, and avoid spending our lives on worthless garbage. We must not lay on someone else the responsibility of filling our days with meaning. I myself must use my days for doing something good, for doing something I need not be ashamed of in the end. But all of us have to work this out proactively for ourselves; we must not allow it to be mercilessly demanded from us by those around us.

We may perhaps put the question like this: "Why should this terrible thing have happened to me of all people?" We might phrase the question like this if we are looking for a scientific, causal explanation. Suppose, for example, that my child comes down with the measles. I want to know what brought it about. I'd like it to be something obvious, thank you very much. We are charmed by clear, black-and-white answers, as if we are bewitched by the connection between cause and effect. But those who offer answers to such questions need to be alert, for sometimes the question is really about *meaning*. Parents of a mentally handicapped child have told me that on first receiving the hard news, they asked exactly this sort of question, but the answer they were given had to do with chromosomes. Information of that kind may eventually be of interest to them, but in those first awful moments, what they are really asking is *why?* Is there any meaning in this?

Sometimes the answer is not scientific at all, but purely superstitious, offering a kind of irrational cause. It wasn't germs, since he didn't have a chill; it was actually the neighbor's nasty children, or a witch with the evil eye. Or we imagine some unobliging Greek god, a vengeful deity who yields us nothing. We might think that this has happened to us simply because we had things too good at the moment.

This kind of thinking has nothing to do with Christian faith. Even less so, if we magnify the superstitious element in searching for a scapegoat, a tendency that seems deeply rooted in us. If my child contracts meningitis—was it my fault? Was I negligent somehow? Did I not love her enough? Or did I love him too much? Or was it the fault of the clinic for not seeing what was there? We want to lay the blame somewhere, whether on ourselves, on someone else, even on God. The simple truth that evil exists and that it strikes wherever it wishes, as it pleases, seems too hard—or too simple—to accept.

Sometimes the question may be only a cry for help, a scream, an expression of despair, a lament—hopefully one made to God. "Absolom, my son, my son!" cried David. "If only I had died instead of you! O Absolom, my son, my son!"

Of course, it is absurd to say "only" in reference to calling out to God. It is precisely our calling out, our complaint, our sense of where we should turn, that opens us up to God's help. And occasionally perhaps, we may be able to lay aside our rationalizing. I once had a devout colleague who suffered from agonizing back pain. We were discussing how we might find a meaning in all our suffering, and he finally said: "But isn't it pretentious of us Christians to insist that our own suffering has to have meaning? Could we not, together with Christ, simply share the meaningless suffering of the rest of the world?"

Heaven Has Twelve Gates

Luke 18:31–43; Rev 21:12; Exod 12; John 19:31–37

Once a blind man sat at the roadside, calling out. Once a bomb fell on a house full of children. Once a young mother screamed as the respirator was removed from a stiffening little body; she screamed and banged her head against the wall. Once a man banged his wife's head against the wall until she dropped to the floor, bleeding from her nose and ears. Once a young man, terrified of dragons and demons that only he could see, backed into a window and fell out of it. Once a car skidded through a crosswalk in front of a school. ENOUGH! I say. I know all this. And it is not just "once"; it happens all the time.

I do not believe that God wills this to happen. No, I am convinced both that God does not will the evil that occurs and that it is not God who lies behind it. I am also convinced that when we accept life as it comes, sharing it with God, something good will come from even the most difficult things that happen to us.

But not before the afflicted acknowledge their sin, right? That is where everything must begin; so we always say, anyway. What a lie that is! Yet we begin worship with our confession of sins and with the prayer "Lord have mercy," sometimes in service sung in the whiniest of church melodies. Should we regard this procedure as taking care of our guilt? It is actually a call for help; the cry of a blind man sitting at the side of the dusty Jericho road! Jesus gives his help, and as far as we can see in the text—not to mention in other texts where he encounters the sick and needy—he requires no confession and he gives no absolution. He finds another way to cure the blind man.

Therefore there must be other ways of meeting God than by exchanging our sins for forgiveness. If I look at my own experience, or if you look at yours, we know that what our hearts are constantly burdened with is not our own stupidity. It is just as likely that our burden will be something like, "God, I'm so tired! I hurt so much! I am so desperately worried about my children! I yearn so deeply for that person I cannot have that I can hardly bear it. My life feels meaningless! I don't know how I can keep going with my work! I am so sick! I am so lonely! I am so sorry! I am so hurt! I am abused, scorned, rejected."

Heaven has twelve gates according to the Book of Revelation. No one knows what they all are, but it seems to me as if our Reformation fixation on sin and guilt opens only one of them. Shouldn't the church—and not just her Lord—usher people in through several of them? Shouldn't we be afraid that in having learned to handle guilt decently and in order, we have failed to deal with oppression, exposure, or shame—the victim's shame? Or perhaps it is not Luther and the Reformers at all who determine our thinking in this, but Freud. Guilt will be forgiven, indeed, but shame must be healed. God takes care of both. Why shouldn't our worship services remind us of this?

Visualize the very first Passover in Egypt, full of hurried, feverish activity. Pack up! Quickly! Get the bread baked and no leaven in the dough! Say goodbye to the neighbors! Keep the children quiet and eat the meal with your backpacks on, ready to go! Blood from a guiltless, select, and faultless victim—a lamb—is applied around the doorframe. An angel of death moves from house to house among the oppressors, slaying and slaying again.

Isn't this what we ask for when we say, "Why doesn't God do anything? Why doesn't God put a stop to oppression?" Or do we find it appalling? Are we shocked by our own impulse to annihilate those who oppose us, those who harm a child in body and soul, those who initiate a war merely to loot the "enemy," merely for the sake of "sordid gain"?

God is there even in slavery, and God makes a way for the victim of oppression. Before long, through baptism in the Red Sea, Israel is born as a nation. Year after year Passover is celebrated with lamb and unleavened bread, and with bitter herbs as a reminder of that bitter time. Gradually it dawns on us: no one is exclusively victim or victimizer. The sacrificial lamb more and more clearly bears the guilt of the people and dies in their place. Thus Passover teaches us that blood saves the one who is ill-treated and oppressed. But the blood also saves the oppressor and the power-monger.

He stayed awake all night that final night in Jerusalem; in no sense did he sleep. He knew what he was doing; he was not a victim of his circumstances. He passed around the bread and wine—"my body broken, my blood poured out." He goes out to share the anguish felt by all who know they face execution at dawn. He accepts treachery with all those who have been betrayed by someone with whom they've broken bread, eaten a meal or shared a bed. Along with all those whose consciences have been driven by God's Spirit in new paths, he is arrested by the police of a self-righteous establishment. He stands before the Great Council and confesses, "Yes, I am the one who shall one day judge you. God is in me. When I go the way of a condemned innocent, God is in me; God is with all those who ever suffer the condemnation of the innocent."

When morning comes, he has not slept. He has eaten and sung the usual hymns, he has prayed and wept, and he has been interrogated before secular and religious courts. He is condemned to death, and the Roman soldiers, anticipating this extra duty as a kind of bonus pay, flog his back with a cat-o-nine-tails. Then he is nailed to the cross, foot and wrist.

It can take a while for a strong man to die by crucifixion, but sooner or later he can no longer raise his body in order to breathe, and he sinks down and suffocates. If time is short, guards can shatter shinbones so that the condemned cannot raise themselves up in order to breathe. These Roman soldiers knew this. The Nazis knew it at Auschwitz. There they didn't want to waste the nails; instead they simply tied people up by their hands and hung them from hooks on the walls until they died. And in the same way as it happened with Jesus, the Nazis found that in a person who died this way, blood and lymph fluid gathered in the lungs and ran out if the person's side was pierced. Thus Jesus was there even in the Nazi torture chambers.

This method of accomplishing the deed is wholly different from the one followed by the Angel of Vengeance in Egypt. It is a way that led down to the vilest thing we human beings could invent, the way to the torturer and his victim. Our God is a God who goes all the way down to them and who sees them both, dying with the victim and dying for the torturer.

God broke up the structures of power and the patterns of behavior built on hatred and force and on the abuse of the power found in strength, knowledge, intelligence, money, gender, and skin color. God broke them up with another model—identification with the victims. It is the model of the lamb, of the blood of the innocent; in it God is able to reach even the oppressor within me, that thing within me that craves power, that sacrifices others so that I can retain or increase that power, that hardens itself in resistance to suffering.

Ash Wednesday

Jas 2:14–17; Isa 58:4–9; Gal 5:22; John 4:14; Luke 5:33–39; 2 Cor 5:17

It's dreary, raining—or maybe not. The typical Lund winter weather cannot make up its mind whether it wants to drizzle or just be foggy. The temperature hovers just above freezing. There is a little ache, a little devil, in each and every muscle. Indecisive light finally appears later on in the short winter day. The clouds lighten up a bit, but there is a chill in the wind when I open the windows to air out the place. But I have to get some fresh air in here! It is so close and suffocating. The room is full of tasks I must do, full of smoke from yesterday and of the musty smell of defeats.

But look at that! I can't believe it! Flowers burst forth with laughter from mere bulbs! My amaryllis is finally blooming, though at Christmas it wouldn't do a thing. What a sermon for Ash Wednesday! This strong, good, uncanny life—will we ever be able to depart from it with thankfulness? Will we be able to think and speak well of it, or must we give up on it? Can we keep joy alive—and curiosity, and love?

Love is what this day is all about. James writes to me: "If a brother or sister is naked and lacks daily food, and one of you says to them, 'Go in peace; keep warm and eat your fill,' and yet you do not supply their bodily needs, what is the good of that?"

Self-evident! Love is not just beautiful words and feelings; it is action. The first shape love assumes is practical care, like wiping a child's nose or mopping the kitchen floor for a sick friend. As Isaiah describes it, "Loose the bonds of injustice, undo the thongs of the yoke, let the oppressed go free, share your bread with the hungry, and bring the homeless poor into your house. . . ."

Yet it makes me feel tired just to hear this, old and tired. The need is endless, both in the world at large and in my own little corner of it. I find myself covering my ears when the TV war correspondents make their reports, and I'm powerless in the face of what I see right here in my neighborhood. I find it hard to keep a grip on the fact that it truly is the small deeds that build the world, and that I must do my little part, but only *my* little part.

The pastor who confirmed me when I was young taught me that there are only three ways of living. A person can be a worthless, empty well, taking in nothing of life's beauty and God's goodness—those who need help will not find it there. Or a person can be like a downspout, something that occasionally needs cleaning out. When God gives forgiveness, joy, peace—what we call grace, it is transformed into practical deeds meeting the needs of others. But that transformation has to happen immediately! Grace is always perishable; it has a shelf life almost as short as milk's. Or, third, a person can be like a rain barrel, taking in what God gives, but only taking it in, never giving it out. A person like this soon sours.

Well, then, let love flow out from me; let it gush! For God's love continually comes to me. I wish I always felt its fire against injustice, its searing heat, hot as a welder's torch. It's all the more difficult, though, just knowing that that fire burns there, somewhere inside me, beneath all the rubbish and fatigue. Sometimes, truly, I must pull myself together. Sometimes the old self in me needs a good scolding: Silence! Back in your place! It's not about you! You don't make the decisions around here!

Nor does it get any easier just because we no longer need to follow old rules. Instead of rules at all, it is now love's imagination that takes over. This creative imagination sees what needs to be done by observing what others need. Only in this way can chains be broken. This is new wine—love's imagination in new wineskins—my faith, my renewed self. I am truly new, even if I feel old.

Perhaps I'll believe the amaryllis today. It's telling me that any day of the year can be Christmas or Easter. There in the amaryllis bulb lie the hope and the strength for the flower. I must hold fast to this. When I struggle to do something good, or when I can't do anything good and struggle just to keep my spirits up, then I'm on the winning side, on God's side. And God is on my side. There is always the coming of spring, full of new life.

The Rightful Lord of All Things

Rev 1:8, 4:8, 11:17, 15:3, 16:7, 19:6, 21:22, 16:14

I believe in God the Father almighty, maker of heaven and earth . . . or do I? Well, it depends entirely on how I read a few of these familiar words. The fact that the word "father" gives many of us a heartfelt feeling of terror or of absence, a feeling we cannot rationalize away, is the lesser problem. As the source of everything, God has been called father—the source of life and energy, children and pussy willows, space and stars, clouds of cosmic dust and planets, the infinitely large and the infinitely small, things that most of us do not understand—quarks and superstrings and dark matter. It is God who created it all and God who draws it all back.

The word "almighty" is more difficult. It represents a three-stage translation, with a slight shift in meaning at each stage. Around the year 140, the Christian congregation in Rome created a baptismal confession that we call the confession of faith (and that we still use today). They spoke Latin and called God *omnipotens*, meaning "the one who is able to do all things" or "the one powerful enough to do anything." But this Latin term is itself a translation from the New Testament Greek word *pantokrator*, which means "the one who has hold of everything" or "the one who rules over everything."

Neither *omnipotens* nor *pantokrator* implies that God is unable to yield some power; nor does either word imply that currently there is no rebellion in progress against that power. Moreover, neither word implies that everything that happens originates with God, though the term "almighty" has increasingly come to be used in that way. But if what we mean to say is that everything that happens does originate with God, then we should instead use an expression like "the cause of all things."

Some people suggest retranslating or reformulating the first article of the creed to the form, "I believe in God, the almighty Father." But that approach would merely cement the antiquated and narrow image that, for most of us, points in the wrong direction. Personally, I'd rather reformulate it like this: "I believe in God, the source and goal of all things and the rightful lord of all things."

We simply cannot cling to pious formulations for their own sake if they do not reflect the content of the New Testament, even more so if they clash with what we know from our experience of the world. Anyone (and sometimes we discover that the anyone includes us ourselves) is justified in crying out in desperation: "This doesn't make sense! If God is god, then he cannot be almighty. But if God is almighty, then he cannot be god." Such a cry bursts from the fact that we must be honest about what we see and know, namely that there is much evil in the world and it often affects us and those we love. It is blindly naïve to say otherwise.

Some people triumphantly point out that there are Old Testament texts teaching that both evil and good come from God, but this does not convince me that God is the *cause* of all things. We must, in fact, accept what we actually do see and read in the Bible—namely that there is variation in the ways in which God is depicted in Scripture. If we believe that we have the full and final revelation of God in Jesus, then we must allow the picture of God that Jesus sets before us to replace all other gods. And for Jesus of Nazareth there is an enemy, a satan, an evil power that opposes God.

The argument that what looks like evil today will, in wider perspective, reveal itself as love, I find equally unconvincing. We recognize love when we see it. God's love is recognized as love in the person of Jesus of Nazareth. We must not say, then, that what is currently painful will gradually be seen to be a blessing, nor that what feels like hatred is in fact the love of God. We have a choice to make. On the one hand we may choose to see God as the cause of all things, as Islam thinks of Allah and the prophets sometimes portray Yahweh. That philosophy requires no evil power in order to be consistent. Everything that happens, happens through this God, and in that case God is, at the very least, appalling. On the other hand, we can understand God's innermost identity as love, love that upholds the universe. This is perhaps what the images of God as a father are about: we are carried like a child in arms. But in that case, God is not alone, and we cannot say that God is the cause of everything that happens.

Evil exists, call it what you like. We must not say that we "believe in it," however, for in terms of the creed, believing in something implies confidence in it, and we must beware of putting our confidence in evil power. But the time for evil is limited. The word *pantokrator* itself does not occur in the New Testament until the Book of Revelation, John's vision of the final struggle, when God will conquer everything at last. The self-designation of the one who speaks there with John is "the Alpha and the Omega, who is and who was and who is to come, the Almighty."

The created beings, the elders, and those who have conquered the beast and its image sing praises to the ruler of all. Even the altar speaks and the voice of the great flock praises God. The heavenly city has no need of a temple, for the Lord God is its temple. This entire remarkable vision deals with the battle on the Lord God's great day.

Although trying to interpret the Book of Revelation in small segments is very risky, what is presented in this portion of it is clearly the same thing that Jesus spoke of in his final days, and that prophets and preachers foretold in the time of both the new and the old covenants. Both Revelation and prophets speak of a final struggle, when the oppressed will be vindicated, when all victims will be set free from their shame, and when all unrighteous wielders of power will be condemned. Then God will at last stand as the sole victor.

Jesus Hangs in Our Hall

John 12:20–23; 1 Cor 13:1–13; Mark 10:32–45

"We wish to see Jesus," some Greeks say to Philip. Right! Who wouldn't? And one day we shall, at a point beyond time, face to face. "For now we see in a mirror, dimly," says Paul, "but then we will see as we are seen by God; then I will know fully, even as I have been fully known by God."

But if Paul means full knowledge about God, then I don't believe him. We will never understand all there is to know about God—only a little more someday. Of course, there are some of us who hope that by observing the church we will be able to see what God is like. Or perhaps we try to see God in those who actually are the church (namely, one another!), or in the churchly institution with all its forms and regimen, buildings and liturgies. This is an all too common and a very serious error; quite likely it is just the reason why the church today is such a hindrance to faith, since so much within the church, and in us who constitute the church, bears no similarity to God.

I know of no harder word of condemnation against the church than the one Jesus speaks en route to Jerusalem. James and John have got it into their heads that they are more worthy of notice than all his other followers. They request therefore that they be given places of honor at the heavenly banquet. The rest of the group did not appreciate this, of course, so Jesus gathers them together. "You know," he says, that "those who are reckoned as rulers lord it over their people, and great ones are tyrants over them. *But it is not so among you.* Whoever wishes to become great among you must be the servant of the others."

These very words echo in my head: "It is not so among you." In fact, it is indeed so, exactly so, no less within the church than outside of it. A morass of hierarchy and lordly airs, salary scales, status seeking, and hysteria over how much we accomplish; it's exactly the way it is. We are willing to serve, perhaps, but not always. This is too often the case if serving becomes difficult, awkward, or demanding, and not at all if our serving won't result in response, feedback, or a better image. A word of condemnation stands over us, the church, in this pronouncement: "It is not so among you." It gives us something to contemplate as we follow the Lord to Golgotha.

A dream I heard of several decades ago remains sharp and clear in my memory. It was like this: "You! Oh you! Come here so I can tell you something! I had a dream, a very strange dream! At first in this dream, everything seemed entirely normal. You certainly know what I mean. Ordinarily I prefer not to talk about it with anyone, but of course you already know. I was at home and Daddy was drunk, as usual. He was completely soused, boisterous, and blubbery.

> *"You remember what our kitchen is like: a long narrow room with a window at one end and a bench under the window. There's a table, too, of course. Momma always says that the table is too big, but actually it's just right. For if you pull it up as close as you can to the bench, you can sort of barricade yourself in. It works well, at least when he is drunk enough, since he stumbles against it and can't get at us. Two of us can huddle side by side like this on the bench, if he's drunk enough, that is. Otherwise we have to decide each time which of us will try to distract him with conversation, or even endure his fists, while the other makes a run for it.*

"It was almost the usual scene again this time, too, in my dream. Daddy was coming after us, and we put up our arms to protect our heads. He was screaming and carrying on about the government and its injustices, about Momma's bad cooking, and God knows what all. When he stumbled once again, Momma bravely jumped in and wrestled him to the floor. It was important to get him quieted down, so as to avoid shaming ourselves in front of the neighbors. So she hushed him like a baby, holding him and shushing him, the old sot.

"I went out into the hall so I wouldn't have to watch or listen to it any more. And, guess what! Jesus was hanging there in our hall. He was hanging on the cross, waiting to die. He didn't say anything, a slight smile perhaps. Blood and tears ran down the deep furrows in his face. I'm sure he felt great pain somewhere, but he looked at me with love. I recognize love when I see it, you know.

"There was nothing especially odd about Jesus hanging there in our darkened hall. It was exactly as it should be. I regarded it as completely natural. But now comes the eerie, frightening part. For at that moment Jesus climbed down from the cross. I saw that he was wearing the same sort of long caftan our pastor wears. And his face suddenly looked as smooth as the pastor's. All those furrows and wrinkles of fatigue were gone, the bloodstains and tears, all gone. He stretched out his hand and it was soft and gentle, exactly as the pastor's. And he smelled of Old Spice—can you imagine? Jesus smelled of aftershave! And he took my hand, smiling in a well-mannered way, and said, 'How nice to see you, little friend. You are well as usual, I suppose? And your sweet little momma, I'm sure she's fine, too.'"

Take Up Your Cross

Mark 8:34–35; Gen 3:12; John 5:30; Col 3:3; John 12:20–33

It's not so simple following Jesus to Jerusalem. What he says is so grave and serious. "If any want to become my followers, let them deny themselves and take up their cross and follow me. For those who want to save their life will lose it, and those who lose their life for my sake, and for the sake of the gospel, will save it."

Why does he talk like this? So much misery has come of the business of self-denial—ashes and self-contempt, passivity and easy deference toward others. Didn't he foresee this? And the cross—he's obviously not talking about a piece of jewelry dangling from a necklace, but an instrument for executing people. In an extended and perhaps less "lethal" sense, the cross also refers to suffering. But is even this something we would take on willingly? It's a question worth thinking about.

Some kinds of suffering we simply get caught up in, of course, just by virtue of being human beings—loneliness, illness, sorrow. Other kinds we bring upon ourselves, perhaps because we are stingy, spiteful, or lazy. But this much we can be sure of: it is never God who sends us suffering. The question, then, is whether there is any sort of suffering we can avoid, and whether we should avoid it, if there is.

Obviously, we should be able to avoid the suffering that comes of our stupidity. If I am unfaithful and insolent to someone, the result may well be that he or she will want nothing more to do with me. If we smoke, or mistreat our bodies in some other way, we had better be prepared to take the consequences. And just consider the catastrophe of destroying the natural world that we ourselves are part of and depend upon for life itself!

Consequences are not the same thing as punishment. Nothing that happens to us comes as a punishment from God. Still, whether we spill milk on the kitchen floor or kill someone while driving in a drunken stupor, or whether our pollutants poison the ground water or our standard of living creates famine in another part of the world—there are consequences, small or severe, to all of these things, either for myself or (in the worst case) for someone else. And whether or not I ask God and my neighbor for forgiveness, I still have to take the consequences. I have to wipe up the milk or do something about the imbalance in the world's living conditions. And I must live with the knowledge of my stupid behavior. There is no solution in trying to wriggle out of it, as Adam did—"It wasn't me! It was her. In fact it was your fault! You gave her to me!"

There is, second, the suffering that maturity always brings us, the suffering that comes when I do my utmost to develop a talent God has given me, the suffering that comes of taking a position on some issue, of being a free, authentic human being who makes choices. We can avoid this kind of suffering, too, merely by forfeiting our privilege, and I think that today's culture in many ways encourages us to do just that. Sometimes the church encourages us in this way as well, since it is easier to deal with people who themselves do not wish to think through the distinctions between right and wrong, but would prefer simply to submit to those in authority; it is easier to herd people who do not wish to use their gifts, consciences, or talents, in order to participate in hard, creative work. Those who fight to preserve orthodoxy, to promote uniformity of culture, or even to establish a dictatorship have an equally strong interest in standardizing human life and keeping people at the level of infants. But none of these things happens with God's approval.

The third sort of avoidable suffering is the kind that comes of confessing Christ in word or deed, when doing so is risky or downright dangerous. It is this suffering that Jesus has in mind when he tells his followers to take up their crosses. Does this mean that Jesus himself brings about suffering? He never uses force. He knows that evil cannot be overcome with evil. He knows that the one who tries to be good in this world, who tries to remain on God's side, will be exposed. He knows that the one who believes can easily end up suffering scorn and persecution. That's just the way it works. If you try to follow Jesus, you open yourself to suffering. It is your cross; it's not something you yourself would choose, as if it were easier or more glamorous than some other option. Take it up, he says. Do not run from faith and goodness, just to avoid suffering. Do not compromise with evil in order to escape being exposed. Do what you know you must do for God's sake, do what you know to be your calling, even if it requires effort and sacrifice.

He also knows that our lives are not our own, that they belong to God, and he knew just as surely that his life was not his own. He had not come to earth to do his own will. He did not come to possess his own life, to help himself to whatever he wanted, or to make himself great at the expense of someone else. Nor did he come to bow to the will of others, no matter how closely related to him they might have been or how important they were. He came not to "go with the flow," to follow common opinion, to comply with a party program, or to cater to group interests. He came instead to do the will of God.

This is what it means to bear one's cross: it means not saying, "It's my life, entirely at my disposal; I can do with it whatever I want; I have a right to take for myself whatever I can get." Instead it means to say, "My life is in God's hands. My life is hidden with Christ in God. I am called to be as much like Christ as I can be, right here in the midst of evil and in spite of the suffering it may bring me."

Christ recognized this as the way of victory, but he saw, too, that it led to victory only through death. "Unless a grain of wheat falls into the earth and dies, it remains just a single grain," he says. I try to take in what this means. Do I have any idea at all what a planted grain of wheat, the mother of an ear of wheat, would look like as the harvest time approaches?

I'll have to check it out next summer. For now, however, I know exactly what a winter potato looks like when it has been left forgotten in the wrong bin. That's the kind of thing that happens when one isn't sufficiently interested in the state of her kitchen! That neglected potato is now shrunken, earth-encrusted, and sporting long sprouts, pale as maggots. "Yuk!" say the grandchildren. "No," grandma answers, this is the mother potato and those are the umbilical cords for the new potatoes. And as usual we go look it up in one of our many nature books.

He is a mother potato, our Master; there is no doubt about it. Jesus must be put into the earth and die, in order to be able to give new life. Like a grain of wheat. And I realize that the same applies to me. The strength and beauty of that full ear of wheat is something I will only see once I have fallen to the earth, once everything has fallen away from me—pride, joy, burdens, pain—and I snuggle up to God with a prayer: "Take me back."

Deserts

In an empty room
from gaping empty hooks
hangs life's emptiness.

The pain has hollowed me out.

I have nothing more to give
and nothing more to say
and nothing more to hold on to.

Everything as slipped its hold on me.

The Emptiness
(Ruth 1:20–21)

The First Bow

Matt 4:1–11; Mark 14:32–42; John 16:12; Luke 13:34

The desert—the scene of his first act—is something I have only seen in nature films. Deserts of sand, deserts of rock . . . and heat, the deadly heat. When I read in Moberg's *The Immigrants* how Christina was so bitterly cold during those first winters in Wisconsin, I got so cold myself I had to get up and put on a sweater. I am well acquainted with the uncompromising nature of cold weather. But I can't quite imagine the blisteringly hot stones in a desert.

A desert can be something else of course, something inward. A workplace where a person is attacked, a love relationship destroyed, a loneliness we did not choose—any harsh, cruel desert light that forces us to look at ourselves. It can force us to reexamine things, preventing us from turning away, from fleeing the fundamental questions, "Who am I?" and "What does God want?" Almost everyone ends up in a spiritual desert after the first passionate experience of God, after the first infatuation. An absence of feelings, an almost intolerable dryness, suggest that I could easily deny the God I have so recently met, the God who has assured me that I can be transformed. Now I feel like a stone again.

Forty days he is there in the Judean desert, and forty is a symbolic number in the Bible, one that often means "on the edge of the unbearable." We recognize ourselves in this: when I reach my limit—then the devil shows up. It doesn't much matter how we imagine it was for Jesus, whether as an inward monologue or as something he saw. Now it's his turn to be pressured as we have been: If you are to do what God wants you to do with your life, you are going to be hungry sometimes, and cold. You will always have to share your bread. Doing what God wants will take its toll on your body. Is it really what you want? And his answer: I will be what God has chosen for me to be, cost me what it may.

Next question. But wouldn't you like to be more than a mere human being, to be like God? You have received power, so why not enjoy the pleasure of showing it off? Think how many people you could intimidate and lord it over!—Or perhaps a temptation harder yet to resist: Wouldn't you like to eradicate leprosy? Or military violence? Or idolatry? Think how much fame and applause you'd receive! And his answer: Do not tempt God. God alone shall be God and Lord. Power must be used only for serving others. People must not use other people for their own ends. No one may use another person as a mere object.

The third question: But can't you compromise? A little cheating here, a little guile there, and the right to retaliate—wouldn't that be kind of nice? Just a little of my devilish methods and all the success in the world will be yours. And his answer: No! Obedience must be total. I shall have no other God beside God. You come as the ruler of this world, but you have no power over me.

And the devil slinks away. Jesus leaves the desert walking tall and with a light heart, like a victor.

A bow arches from that day in the desert to the night in the old garden outside Jerusalem. Imagine a rainbow such as a child draws, with bright bands in various colors one over the other. This rainbow has only two or three colors, and the innermost bow begins in the desert and comes down in Gethsemane.

What was it like there in the garden? It is difficult to express, for there are scarcely words to describe the hours of his despair. This anxiety has no dimensions to it, no up or down, no before or after, only a horrifying now that wants to swallow me up, kill me, obliterate everything I was and am and said and did and wanted. And most of those around me fall asleep—unless they try to offer something to help me sleep, a calming injection or a soothing assurance. He was there on the ground under the ancient trees and it was night. It was earth and sighing leaves, and perhaps a bird called out. Did he find some kind of security in the very ground, the mold that his blood and sweat dropped upon?

I sometimes think I'd like to die in autumn, so that Stig Dagerman's[4] verse could be used in my obituary. It comforts me and fits my own view of death. Could such thoughts have comforted him?

> *How quickly yellow the maples*
> *that brighten our walk through the park.*
> *To die is to travel the scanty distance*
> *from branch to the firmness of earth.*

Doubtless, there on the ground beneath the trees, he still believed that God would be his firm ground even in death. He has his faith still. But there is still so much to do, too. The evening before, he had said to his disciples: "I still have many things to say to you, but you cannot bear them now." He wept over Jerusalem: "How often have I desired to gather your children together as a hen gathers her brood under her wings, and you were not willing!"

He had had such incredibly little time, between two and three years at most. He had no access to the media, no email, and no cell phone. Yet he devoted an irrationally large amount of time, as it seems, to individuals one by one, to a blind man, to a grieving mother—and he spent long evenings at parties instead of arranging to speak at mass meetings. It was too soon; it's always too soon to snuff out the flame, to stop working for God, to leave loved ones behind, to cease living. He weeps, he screams, he prays, he wants company in his misery. His eyes are bloodshot—we've all been there at one time or another.

He yields himself. This time, too, it is God's will that must prevail, not his own, regardless of what it costs. But this time he does not walk away straight and tall from the temptation, bright and ready for the day's work. This time he is tired—it is night; it's been some time since he's had any sleep, and he'll never sleep again. He's bleeding, he's utterly worn out, but he doesn't flinch as he steps forward to meet the soldiers.

Do you see the rainbow? It's not the bow of thunder and storm beginning in temptation and ending in temptation, but the bow of the promise arching from obedience to obedience.

A Play about Jesus

Mark 1:9–11; Ps 2:7; Isa 42:1–3; Matt 4:1–11; Mark 14:32–43;
Mark 15:34; Luke 2:41–51

If we were to put on a play about Jesus, we could use that rainbow we drew with only a couple of colors. The first scene would
deal with the baptism at the Jordan. There would be flowers and an
intense, warm light, and John the Baptist wearing second-hand
clothes. Those in the crowd would be nobody special, just people
like you and me, people with shabby private lives, broken bodies,
and broken marriages, and a little too much alcohol on their breath.
At first they would be quiet and suspicious.

Does Jesus really need John's baptism, something that was intended for the forgiveness and betterment of sinners? No, it was more
like carrying out an act of solidarity, as in joining a trade union or a
professional society when one owns a business. John baptizes him in
the waters of the river—more light. And then some arrangement to
show that Jesus is sure about what God wants. A voice—from above?
Perhaps a dove, which we recognize as the Holy Spirit? But we must
be circumspect here; it is all too easy for the sublime to become ridic-
ulous. We need careful directions and a well thought-out set design.

"You are my beloved son."

It is a royal title—how can we make it clear for the audience, as
clear as it was for those originally standing there, people who were
well acquainted with the Psalms?

"He is my chosen one."

Same problem. Anyone who has read it or heard it read recalls Isaiah: "Here is my servant, whom I uphold, my chosen, in whom my soul delights; I have put my spirit upon him; he will bring forth justice to the nations. He will not cry or lift up his voice, or make it heard in the street; a bruised reed he will not break, and a dimly burning wick he will not quench."

We could make the crowd function here as a chorus that sings this song of the Lord's Servant, that in yet another way expresses its yearning and expectation. Some kind of dance perhaps, in which people try to draw him into a triumphal march. But he walks away from them; a light surrounds him, but he is quite alone. There beside the Jordan begins the outer rainbow.

Scene Two of our play is of course the desert scene with the temptation. A little trickier, undeniably, but we need to get at the meaning behind this one too. For he was a human being, just as we are, and as long as we are reasonably human, open and willing to learn, we will be able to understand, perceive, to yearn for what he did, for what he wanted. Cold, revealing light can be used here, with heavy, dark, flickering shadows. Jarringly discordant music until he exits victorious and the light becomes warm again, and the music changes tone. There begins the inner rainbow.

Next in the play, two new scenes corresponding to the first two, but now almost total darkness. First, in the garden where the inner bow comes down. Night—we can see almost nothing. On a hill a little distance off: three sleeping disciples. In weak light, but speaking aloud in the middle of the set: Jesus himself. Ancient trees and stars painted on the flats at the back of the stage. He is weeping, he cries out for a way to escape. To escape the nails, to escape offering only silence when he is struck or spit upon. Just to slip away, perhaps.

Yet his prayer comes down to a final "not what I want, but what you want," and that is victory. Perhaps even now there is relief in his voice as he wakens the disciples. Focus bright light on the scene, torches, lanterns—should we have another bright triumphal victory scene? No—for there are soldiers now, his seizure, the violence, the flight of his closest companions—sleeplessness, weariness, his being handed over to hostility, apathy, and barbarity.

He goes to Golgotha, toward absolute isolation: "Eloi, Eloi, lema sabachthani? My God, my God, why have *you* forsaken me?" Here is the termination of the outer bow. It arches from the baptism, where God speaks, to the cross, where God is silent.

There can be a third bow, in addition to the other two. If so, it begins much earlier, in the temple when his mother and father finally find him on the third day. They are dead-tired and exhausted from crying, with nothing but a despairing hope in body and soul. And Jesus upbraids them! "Didn't you know? Didn't you know where I had to be?" The NRSV translates his words, "I must be in my Father's house." But this doesn't quite reflect the underlying Greek text. A more literal rendering would perhaps render it as, "be compelled to be in what is my Father's." We could put it like this: "I must be near the Father; I am compelled to run the Father's errand."

His errand in the world is this: in his person and his life, in what he says and does and in what he is, to show what a true human being must be like, *and* what God is like—what God is like toward us here on the earth, not in eternal glory and blessedness. Both God and human. We tend to visualize Jesus as half and half. But he bore the divine nature in all its fullness within himself. At the same time he was fully and completely human, with a will to do good as well as a desire to be lazy or ill tempered, or to retaliate. In each situation he had to let his good will prevail in order to be a true human being. He was not allowed to use his divine power to show off his cleverness or to rescue himself—he was only permitted to use it to help other people.

This outermost bow, the one that begins with the twelve-year-old's clear voice—does it come down in the dawn of the resurrection morning? I believe it does. There is no logic to it: if he was to run the Father's errand in all respects, he would have to conquer Satan, death, and evil. When a child asks me why it turns out this way, I can only answer, "That's just the way it is." And that is likely the only answer we can take for ourselves, too.

But in some way, his very obedience to what he had to do and be is a key. He knew it so heart-wrenchingly early in his life, and so the outermost bow rises from his brilliant conversation with the scholars in the temple and descends into a grave—into the blinding light from out of that grave. So bright is that light that we must shut our eyes and through closed eyelids merely sense what is happening.

The Horrific Obedience

Gen 1:26–27; Isa 6:1–2; Gen 12:1–4; Luke 1:38; Phil 2:5–11

Week after week for more than a decade, various groups—mostly women, young and old, theologians and others—met at my home so that we could "get to know ourselves and each other, to understand and articulate our faith." We discussed everything. A couple of issues came up again and again: "If you say the word 'obey' one more time, I'm going to throw up!" and "How could he be both completely God and completely human?"

One memorable evening we linked these two questions together:

"What do you think of when someone mentions obedience?"

There were many answers, all clashing with each other.

"I think of blind obedience. Like the Nürmberg trials and people who excused themselves because they had merely obeyed orders. Like rules in a high school. Like an English boy's school."

"So, obedience is a nasty word. Is there any such thing as good obedience?"

"Well, sure! If the house is burning and a fireman says, 'Jump!' then I imagine I'll obey. Kids certainly need to learn that there are rules that apply in society, especially if they want to visit Grandma! And what about traffic laws? And of course we can't carefully explain our concerns

to a three-year-old who finds a box of matches. And we have to obey our conscience, don't we."

"This business of doing what we must do, does that have anything to do with obedience?"

"Are you talking about obeying your destiny? Like an artist?"

"No, I'm talking about becoming what we must become."

"Becoming what God wants us to become? An alternative way of self-actualization? The sort of thing that in the gray hours of dawn we realize that we've never attained?"

"But what about Jesus? Was that blind obedience? Did he get his orders from God gradually, step by step?"

"No, he had to struggle, of course."

"Struggle? With his conscience? To find the truth? But he was God, wasn't he? Wasn't it just automatic for him to do the right thing?"

"Of course not! Otherwise he wouldn't have needed to weep in Gethsemane. Yet weep he did! He struggled like any ordinary person; that's what so beautiful about it. The difference is, of course, that he succeeded in his struggle every time, unlike me."

His success in becoming what God wanted him to become, in doing what God wanted him to do, that's what we can call obedience. A good obedience. Stranger still, by obeying and permitting the will of God to have its way in him clean and clear, he became a true person. He became the only true person of the sort envisioned when God said, "Let us make humankind in our image, according to our likeness." Now at last we see what a true person is really like. And when he obeyed God and made God's will clear, we were also enabled to see what God is like. Not in pure holiness, which is lucky for us, nor are we enabled to see the seraphs, nor the mantle that fills the temple, nor the secrets that lie behind creation. Jesus made it possible instead for us to see what God is like toward us. So strange! When Jesus the human being becomes obedient to what God wants with him, he becomes the true human, the likeness that shows us God. Human and God; God and human.

Obedience is a key word. God called Abraham out from his secure way of life. Abraham heard the command, obeyed it, and set out from his hometown, leaving behind family and friends. And thus began the first covenant. The first thing God needed in order to become a human being was a momma, and she became obedient and gave up assurances of safety. It was a requirement for the new covenant. She said to the angel, "Let it be with me according to your word." So like the words uttered on that last night: "Not what I want, but what you want."

We pray in a contemporary kyrie: "Lord, you became our brother; you understand our need. You bore it all upon your cross. Give us now your salvation." We sing in a hymn by Olof Hartman,[5] "You who went before us, into deepest anguish." One way we can focus our thoughts is on how Jesus goes down ever deeper into our humanity. He came down from his heavenly glory to the little outbuilding where he was born. He continues his descent all the way to helplessness, and he sets aside all outward power.

We can work in the same way with the word "power" as we have done with the word "obedience."

"What do you mean by 'power'? Power brokers, abuse of power, powerless . . . ?"

"Is there such a thing as good power?"

"Sure. Being alongside in making decisions about worthwhile, constructive things. Power to help, perhaps. One can also make *good* use of power, you know, and not just abuse it."

Jesus had God's power to forgive, to heal and to recreate; he had the power that personal integrity always generates, power that allows him to stand tall before judges and executioners. But his helplessness likewise had to be great, as when he was an infant refugee and when he was condemned to death, expelled from the society of the pious, and executed. When we see him using his power to help, but never to aggrandize himself, never to retaliate, then we see once more the sort of person we would like to have for a friend, for our brother. This is a *true* human being. And we see what God's power looks like. God and humanity are joined together within him. Not half of each, but a single, genuine human person, and simultaneously God's power, will, and love laid bare.

Philippians 2:5–11 deals with the mystery of obedience. Paul has adopted an earlier text, written some twenty-five years after Jesus' death—and thus the oldest thinking we have on how Jesus won his victory. It is a text that makes it impossible for me to sidestep these difficult words, "obedience" and "powerlessness."

> *Though he was in the form of God,*
> *he did not regard equality with God*
> *as something to be exploited,*
> *but emptied himself,*
> *taking the form of a slave,*
> *being born in human likeness.*
> *And being found in human form,*
> *he humbled himself*
> *and became obedient to the point of death*
> *—even death on a cross.*

> *Therefore*
> *God also highly exalted him*
> *and gave him the name*
> *that is above every name,*
> *so that at the name of Jesus*
> *every knee should bend,*

in heaven and on earth and under the earth,
and every tongue should confess
that Jesus Christ is Lord,
to the glory of God the Father.

Once, the only time I was down in the catacombs of Rome, it became suddenly clear to me that this is how it had to be. It was one of those insights that a person might wake up with or be gripped by, but which is difficult to formulate or describe to anyone else.

It had to do with the direction in which things move. Down here on the sewer walls someone had drawn a fish, a mute and absurd little creature. Here below ground, in the darkness of persecution, his symbol shows up: the fish. In Greek: *ichthys*, an acronym for "iesous christos theos [h]yios soter": Jesus Christ, God's Son, Savior. It spoke to me across the centuries of dogma. "Exactly!" I said to myself. It had to be exactly this way. Savior—from below. It would have been impossible any other way.

Empty Eyes

1 John 1:5; John 9:1–3; Gen 50:20; Luke 13:10–17; Luke 22:31–32; Matt 13:24–30; Rev 22:2; John 14:30; Luke 10:17–20

I asked another older pastor, who, like me, had endured pain for decades, how he put up with it. I got an instant reply. "Never think that it is your fault or that it's God who has sent it—otherwise you'll go mad." He is absolutely right. This business of being sick sometimes makes it feel as if my body is the enemy, something to fight and perhaps to overcome. The next stage very easily becomes self-hatred, in which I blame myself for becoming ill in the first place. But it is not my fault.

Neither is it God's fault, just as my colleague said to me, for God is the giver of all good gifts, and pain does not qualify as a good gift! "God is light and in him is no darkness at all"; nothing evil comes from God. Well, then, what *is* to blame? I look for the answer in what Jesus said on the subject.

"Who sinned, this man or his parents, that he was born blind?" Jesus' friends asked him one time. Jesus seems to answer about as quickly as my friend did. "Neither this man nor his parents sinned; he was born blind so that God's works might be revealed in him." Well then, sickness is not a punishment, but this leads us to another question: Do some people get sick just so that they can be healed by a miracle? I don't know, but I do consider it more likely that God uses a difficult situation in order to create something grand from it. Just as Joseph in Egypt once said to his brothers, who were frightened out of their wits that he was about to avenge himself on them: "Even though you intended to do harm to me, God intended it for good." You wanted to do me evil, but God has turned it to something good.

One day he was teaching in a synagogue on the Sabbath. There was a woman there who had suffered eighteen years from such a crooked back that she could not straighten up. Jesus delivers her and sets her free to be thankful, but the pious come with their pious objections.

"It is still the Sabbath! Couldn't this have waited?"

"No," replies Jesus. "It has come not one day too soon. Eighteen years is a long time, and that's how long this daughter of Abraham has been kept bound by Satan."

Now it is the final evening, and he knows his friends well enough; he knows what they are about to go through. "Tanning," we used to call it, as with preparing leather. I've never seen the process, so it isn't an image I can easily visualize. "Must she be dragged through the mill again?" a mother asked regarding her young daughter who had been severely afflicted yet another time. It's a question that makes good sense to me. Going through the mill, that's exactly what would happen to the disciples that night. Although Jesus expressed it to Peter like this:

"Simon, Simon, listen! Satan has demanded to sift all of you like wheat!"

It is not God who turns the mill; it is Satan. God prays that we can endure it. "I have prayed for you," he says, "that your own faith may not fail." The millstone is heavy. Heavier yet is the idea that God wants it that way; it's an idea we are not required to believe.

And why doesn't the good seed come up clean and unmixed where the kingdom of heaven is to grow? Where do these weeds come from? It's a justified question from the audience. "An enemy has been here," he tells them. The church, the congregation, looks the way it does, with long-rooted weeds and brilliant blossoms growing side-by-side until the harvest day. We must live with it for now. And give thanks for it, too, for who knows whether I myself might not be pulled out? I am both wheat and quack grass.

He, however, is a tree, a tree that is a cross, which is itself a tree of paradise, whose leaves are for the healing of the nations. Just before he goes out into the darkness that last evening, he says so: "The ruler of this world has no power over me. He has nothing in me." There is one person, at least, over whom Satan has no power—it is truly remarkable.

Yet sometimes Jesus is optimistic even about his own followers. During this journey, as he welcomes back the seventy-two he had sent out, he rejoices. "I watched Satan fall from heaven like a flash of lightning." But right away he realizes that the disciples need to be reminded of the one needful thing, so that they will not focus on their own deeds. "Do not rejoice at this, that the spirits submit to you, but rejoice that your names are written in heaven."

He speaks about Satan, the enemy, an un-god who stands behind everything evil and is well skilled in all manner of destruction: illness, despair, apostasy. What are we to believe then? Are we to believe in the devil, a personal devil? Is there a core in the world's evil, a kind of willing, acting central core?

Christians entertain widely diverse opinions on this matter. We may periodically experience a state of such chaos and violence in the world that there seems to be some sort of evil will lying behind it, driving it all. Other times it is most natural to experience evil fundamentally as mere nothingness, a negation.

I mostly visualize evil as a web, a sticky web cast over the world. (However, I do not think of Satan as a spider! I do not regard spiders as nasty; I actually find them quite interesting!) Everything is interconnected with everything else in this web. It will not do to select our favorite sins—let us all examine ourselves!—and to say: "Thank you! I'll take this one, a little greediness and a little tendency to be scornful and a little grumpiness. I'll leave the rest (which is most of it) for others to claim."

It's like when schoolboys protest, "It wasn't me! Don't blame me for the dirt in the hallway! I brought in a little glob maybe, but it wasn't that much!" As long as we do evil or wish evil or see evil and simply accept evil, we play a role in keeping the web of evil in place over the world. There is no way we can safely carve off a tiny piece to acknowledge and absolve ourselves from the rest.

I think my friend Charlott grasped evil's essence best when as a young theologian she was writing her final paper on that very subject. She often dropped in to discuss it. Is there a will, a driving volition at the core of evil? Is evil something personal, like God? One day she found the solution. "Lena, now I know what the core of evil looks like. It is emptiness. The kind of emptiness we see in the mirror in our own eyes when we have betrayed the one we love."

The Day the Darkness Wants Me

Exod 14:8–15; Rom 8:26–27; Ps 73:23; Rev 21:23

Temptation. It's one of those words that have become trivial and banal. A temptation is a forbidden pastry in a weight-loss program, a new kind of snack in an absurd television commercial.

In the desert story we meet temptation of an entirely different dimension. There a man is pressured to the end of his endurance to give up what he knows he must do. If he succumbs, he betrays God and loses his very self. Or to put it the other way around, he loses God and betrays everything he is and all that he believes in.

But I will do well to guard myself against both the petty and the heroic. Neither one is God's word rising up to say to me: This concerns you! Instead, what gets to me is Luther's explanation to the prayer, "lead us not into temptation." There he speaks of "false belief, despair, and other great and shameful sins." For years I have mulled over these words, turning them this way and that. They are so strange! What on earth can the old monk mean by them?

Then I begin to see that Luther is perhaps speaking of the same thing that Nathanael Beskow[6] speaks of: "The evil day is drawing near for me, the day when the darkness wants me," lines from a hymn that long ago in childhood lodged themselves fast in my head and in my heart. The day the darkness wants me—of course I know exactly what that is. The day I want to give up. The day I capitulate to despair.

Of course, no one escapes this sort of thing, not one of us. Every human being loses someone, fails at something, or is disappointed at some point in life. Every single one of us breaks a promise, blows an opportunity, or grows hard-hearted. When we are hit with illness or loneliness, with malicious gossip or violence or financial hardship— you name it—then the questions come. Why did this have to happen to *me*? What does God mean by it? I believe that the despair Luther speaks of and the darkness Beskow is so familiar with are temptations latent in all the adversity and pain we encounter. They tempt us to abandon God when the darkness falls. They tempt us severely.

One could say that evil comes in two stages. First I get sick, or perhaps I fail at something, or whatever it might be. By itself, any of these is bad enough. But it becomes genuinely worse when I desert God because of it. The Tempter knows this, and so he comes with many good suggestions about how things really ought to be.

Perhaps I begin thinking that God has sent me this sickness as a punishment, though of course I know that Jesus rebuffs all thought of retributive judgment. Still, perhaps I begin going over all my faults and shortcomings, making a mental list of the ones that would definitely merit God's punishment. I begin to believe in a God who has no intention of forgiving me, but who actually wants to see me in this predicament, a God who is not like the Father of Jesus Christ, a God who is easy to hate and to disavow. Disbelief moves in with me. When I give in to such thoughts as these, thoughts that God does not wish me well, then the hour of despair has arrived. I am at risk of going lost.

Or perhaps I begin thinking I must be polite to God, saying only "thanks" and "amen" and "would you kindly do me just a couple small favors." But there are times when I simply need to scream. The Bible is full of screaming, especially in the Psalms. God tolerates *all* our feelings. The important thing is that contact is not broken. To keep despair from seeping in or washing over me like a flood, I must draw God into my suffering. In fact, this is what God wants: to hear our complaint and to be close to us. And when the screaming stops, when words fail us, then at last there is emptiness and silence where God can find room.

All this became especially significant for me when my sister-in-law was battling cancer some years ago. Many of us were praying for her, praying that she might find a way out of this illness. Sometimes, though, I just couldn't pray; it all seemed too difficult and depressing. Moses was once in the same situation, when there did not appear to be any way out, when he saw nothing but a dead end before him. No matter what he chose to do, it would be the wrong thing. He had brought the people out of Egyptian captivity, and now they stood at the edge of the impassible Reed Sea. Pharaoh's troops were right on their tail, and before them lay deep, dark waters. Moses comforted the people, but he himself did not pray—it was simply one of those moments when one does not have the strength for it. And yet, God says to him, "Why do you cry out to me?" How can God say this? Luther explains in his commentary that in such situations as this the Spirit prays within us, and prays so loudly that God must ask, "Why are you shouting at me?"

When we are afflicted with sickness or some other suffering, there are two ways to conquer it. The one is to be set free from the evil, an evil that strikes blindly, at random. That actually does happen—people do get cured after all—and when it happens, it is a victory for Christ. The other way of overcoming is more like the model Christ himself gave us: in the midst of the evil thing, through it in fact, we hold fast to God who never abandons us, who makes the Spirit to pray within us. That's the way Christ went; it's the way in which he led Inga-Lill. She reached her Sea of Reeds ahead of us. The waters opened before her, and she passed through unscathed to the land where "the glory of God is its light, and its lamp is the Lamb."

A Boundary for the Waters

Rev 12:7–12; 1 Pet 5:8; Ps 104; Job 38:1–42:6; Gen 1:1–2:3; Gen 2:4–3:24; Ps 8; Col 1:15–20

I would like to know where evil comes from. Well, no, actually, I probably no longer worry about that. What good would it do me to know? Evil is always there anyway, and it has to be opposed and endured. The Bible doesn't give me any answer. The Bible is so pragmatic! We learn how we can get to heaven and how we should tolerably conduct ourselves along the way. But there are many questions to which we get nothing but silence for an answer.

There is a myth about a fallen angel, but it is a Jewish, extra-biblical tradition and offers no particular clarity on the issue. The story in the Book of Revelation about Michael and the dragon is likewise extremely difficult to penetrate, except in its message that evil, that ancient serpent, prowls around among us, roaring, doing whatever he can to seduce and destroy us. But this doesn't help us either.

In any case, I want to know more about my place as a human being between God and Satan. So I go to the most magnificent of creation texts, Psalm 104. Humanity doesn't get much space there, as a matter of fact. The human is just a praise-singer among hyraxes[7] and storks, winds, and young lions: "I will sing to the LORD as long as I live." Yet evil too appears to be there from the beginning, in the image of a primordial deep, of waters of chaos; they flee at God's roaring, and God sets boundaries for them.

Almost as awesome is the description in the final chapters of Job. Here God uses creation as an argument against Job—exactly how he does this is difficult to grasp, but we can see that the tone is sarcastic, almost ironic: "Where were you when I laid the foundation of the earth? Tell me, if you have understanding."

And when God has finished talking, Job gives up, puts his hand over his mouth and says nothing more. Perhaps he realizes that he has wrongly framed his question about the suffering of the righteous, since he has spoken of God in human categories. But God is God and not a human being. Maybe like many of the psalmists he thinks that God has both power to create and power to save, so that if God can take care of the one, then God can take care of the other as well. I don't know what Job is thinking, nor is there anyone else either who has come to a definitive reading or understanding of Job. But here too, evil is present from the beginning, in the same way as it is in Psalm 104, as a sea with powerful waves, a sea around which God sets a hedge or a boundary, a sea that God shuts up with gates and barriers.

If I turn to the Bible's first pages I see clearly mythical features in the two accounts found there. Myth, of course, does not mean saga; rather it means an account that visualizes a moral insight or that says something about the meaning of life or about God's nature, or about a person's inmost being. In both these creation narratives, evil is present from the beginning as an unexplained entity, portrayed with various kinds of images. In the first account we have the darkness and the great waters; in the second account, a sterile barrenness and immediately God's instructions to what is "not-God." In the first myth, God calls forth light and sets a boundary for the waters. In the other myth, God is portrayed as thinking about what the empty barrenness, the dead landscape, needs, and the solution the Creator arrives at is rain and humanity. In this way the human race becomes a shield against evil. In this way, creation is brought forth as a way to bring order out of chaos, conquering it in battle. But still we find no answer to the question of evil's origin.

What about humanity, then? In Psalm 104 the human creature is merely one part of a whole, in Job's book humanity is portrayed as a knucklehead. In the myth of the seven days, humanity is created male and female in the image and likeness of God. But this is astounding! How is it that we are like God? It certainly isn't that we are eternal or invisible, but we are indeed able to love, to forgive, and to work like God does. And to a certain degree we are able to understand God's love, forgiveness, and work. Human beings are also unfathomable as God is. Psalm 8 gives us the same exalted picture: "You have made them a little lower than God." And it is in precisely these accounts that we get the idea that humanity is to rule over all the rest of creation.

Of course, this has shown itself to be dangerous statement, both for the earth and, in the end, also for us. We plunder, exploit, and destroy, as if the word "rule over" gave us license to do so. The Church has tried to speak instead of trusteeship and responsibility. But when these ancient texts originated, neither plunder nor trusteeship was a possibility for this little nomadic people, barely established in Canaan. Most likely the meaning was first understood as parallel to the first commandment: "You shall have no other gods before me." Surrounded as they were by cultures that regarded the sun, moon, and stars as divinities and by peoples who prayed at wells and trees to gods fashioned in the form of animals, the nation received this reply: God alone is to be God. You are to pray to nothing else. Nothing else is to be your lord. Everything belongs to God's creation, even you.

So what happens? Humanity, in its majesty resembling God, being made almost a god, a shield against evil, forfeits its majesty and allies itself with Satan. Adam—and we are all Adam—abandoned his assigned role and opened himself up to disobedience, self-assertion, and the making of excuses. He would become perpetually hesitant, always double-minded, always belonging to God, but always in hock to the devil.

We have therefore been handed a possibility of sorts for making a choice. We were not compelled to obey God or to live together with God. This may perhaps be related to the fact that God's very nature is love, that God wants to be loved in return by those who choose to do so. If that's the case, we can understand it. We delight in a dog's great love and tolerance, and in the trust and devotion of small children. But the love we value most is when one who is utterly free and could say "no" decides to stay beside us and love us.

That's not to say that we are always free to choose. A good part of each of us has been injured along the way; much of what motivates us is subconscious, and there are thus destructive patterns within us that often guide us. Nor does it mean that it is necessarily simple to choose between black and white. The older we get, the clearer it becomes that we live in a world of grays, where at times all solutions are somehow bad solutions.

Is there any comfort in this? Indeed there is, for in Christ all things in heaven and on earth were created, things visible and invisible. He himself is before all things, and in him all things hold together. There is thus a pervasive pattern, a design for all creation: it is the love that gives of itself. There is a model for our lives, for our striving in the midst of the grays; it is the possibility of establishing peace and of reconciling everything through him and to him.

We Cannot Own Peace

Ps 91; Matt 24:27

It looks like it will be a lovely day. Bright sun and fresh air. I slept well the entire night; those who understand what that means will understand; I have no way to explain it to those who do not. Perhaps I'll last through nearly the whole day, rather than just a few hours, or not at all, as often happens otherwise. Maybe it will be a "star day," and not merely "star hours," as Ninni refers to them, Ninni who is far sicker than I am.

Midsummer's eve in the mid-1970s, Ninni and I sat on beds in a youth camp bunkhouse and drank claret. We had slipped away from the rest of the group and their celebration, and to be candid we didn't consider it any great loss. We thought that we knew so much more about life than all those other assured, complacent people—though we could have given that a bit more thought! Both of us were in the early stages of our illnesses, neither of us having had a diagnosis, and so it was easy for people to say about us, "It's only nerves."

We wrote a couple poems there in the bunkhouse on that lovely night; I thought of them again when I came across Psalm 91 in the new prayer book. It also appears in one of the evening prayers of the missal, in the Sunday complines. It makes big claims full of pious expectations. "God will deliver you from the snare of the fowler. . . . You will not fear the terror of the night . . . or the pestilence that stalks in darkness. . . . No evil shall befall you, no scourge come near your tent."

It turned out to be something more complicated than pestilence that smote Ninni, and something as uncomplicated as pain that struck me. One may well wonder whether the psalmist—or later preachers who imitate him—really believe what they say. We didn't think so. Of course, we were younger back then, but already we knew a lot about losing something. We would know more soon enough.

But we also knew that the psalmist was partly right. "You will tread on the lion and the adder"—right, and we feel their bite in every joint—"the young lion and the serpent you will trample under foot"—right, I suppress despair and exhaustion with every available means, including claret—"God will be with me in trouble"—right! But that is whole other matter.

This is the first poem we wrote:

Safety is found in the things we can own:
house and home, health, welfare,
money, future and a good reputation.
Everything we are fond of and hold on to,
what we grasp with our greedy hands
runs like sand between our fingers.
Safety lies in whatever we can lose.

Peace we cannot own.
But when we give it all up
and possess as if we did not possess
or when we have forfeited everything
and stand there naked in the storm
or have lost every grip
and fallen headfirst toward God—
then peace can own us.

I feel like crying for a moment over what we were then; I'd like to have done something to shield us from what was coming, both from the disease itself and from the parties put on by those safe people, as well as from all the slanderous assurances that neither of

us was really sick. But that long ago night we did not feel we needed
protection, other than from God perhaps. Instead we felt a sort of
pride. We began speculating whether suffering might perhaps be
apportioned out only to a select few, speculating whether for some
inscrutable purpose God intended to lay more of it on some than
on others. We instantly felt as if we were in the same class with
John the Baptist. And so we wrote another poem, this one for John
the Baptist's day.[8]

> *He lets some of us lie down in green pastures.*
> *Some must live in Transjordanian deserts*
> *or in ordinary Swedish swamps.*
>
> *O homeland! Where the ground quakes,*
> *where fog dwells and darkened water fills up holes.*
> *Give me the land filled with intoxicating scents of bayberry,*
> *wide horizons, open sky,*
> *a home for giant birds!*
>
> *Now that I've found this firm turf to walk on,*
> *I'll stay right here and call*
> *to those who must come after me along the selfsame way:*
>
> *Step lively! Do not let your foot*
> *rest long in any single spot.*
> *If you sink, do not fight it.*
> *For then, either help is near*
> *or the end of agony—darkness good and soothing.*
>
> *Immediately beyond the worst of waters*
> *a plank is laid*
> *to reach dry sand and blooming heather.*
> *Drop down upon the firm and stable ground*
> *and wait expectantly for the first glint*
> *that sparks the flash of lightning*
> *from the east as far as the west.*

Even today I don't rightly know how it works with choosing who must suffer. Yet still today I'm waiting for that flash of lightning—translate it as thunderbolt if you like, but Ninni and I both saw for ourselves how it danced along the hilltops.

And if he does not come in fire before the darkness overtakes one of us, I know that a day is coming when the serpent's time will be over, the good and soothing darkness will enfold us to its breast, like someone lifting us out of the weeping and the evil dreams of the night.

Israel and Jacob

The nights are spent
picking at sores
that have healed badly.

The examiner's scalpel
makes a new incision
among illusions and things forgotten.

Conversion
(Joel 2:13)

You Israel, You Jacob

Isa 44:21–22; Gen 32:22–31; Phil 2:9; Rev 14:1

you Israel you Jacob
it is me a human being
who is addressed with this double name
a human being who bears duality division
split right down through her very essence day and night

Jacob the traitor
he who came after
who desired to go before
who connived his way into the inheritance
who betrayed his brother
the one he had played with and trusted
before the boundaries of the self became much too distinct

Israel the Lord's warrior
he who wants God's ways
who strives for the right
who stands up for the good
who stands in solidarity with justice
and who wants to belong to the kingdom of God
here at a ford a passage he gets a change of name
no not a change but an addition
so that my self-image becomes more complete

one sends so much on ahead to soften God up
one offers him what one can
and it can take all of one's possessions
isn't that enough
to guarantee that my life is spared
so that I can perhaps keep it for myself
control it as if it were my own
as something I'm entitled to

I send my own family
even they must finally go, they who are
my most vulnerable point
even they are part of my offering to him
see here my community my relationship my life
my entire earthly life
just take it if it means I escape
but I do not escape

and it takes a night and yet another night
in fact the crossings are many
and I must stay awake and wrestle
and the angel seldom shows his face and keeps silence until the morning

but the message is clear
you must give up your life
your desire to make excuses
somewhere it must be given up
you must fall into his hands
for a moment be healed
escape your burden lay it down by the riverside here right here
collapse for a moment into a single identity
and then for your remaining days go around lame in the hip
a bit less fit for normal life
normal community normal coherent talk about God
rational discussion and religious duties
handicapped from wrestling all night long

and transgressions are swept away like mere clouds and morning mist
yet the morning mist can be damp and cold for the soul
and the demons of the dawn are among life's worst
demons of the dawn that squatted under Gethsemane's trees
where another entity was created
where a new name come forth
the name above all names
when the last thing of all was given up
the right to one's own life
when long ago possessions and family had been sent on ahead
the only thing left to lose was one's own life

the Lord keeps us together as a unit
sees the unity within us as he wanted us
helps us to survive disintegration
in his mercy his warm blessing
when the sun breaks through
we can perhaps more and more be healed and made well
and become integrated centered
forfeit fragmentation and multiplicity
gain the simple heart

there is one more name
an invisible name written on the forehead
a name that he alone knows
a name beyond traitor and warrior
a name for rest and unity and totality

but for now the split will always be painful
the cleft between what I am and what I want to be
between what I am and what I also am

The Double Appellation

Isa 44:21; Gen 32:22–31; Isa 44:1–2; John 19:5

Sometimes I think it's because of being middle-aged that I am so seldom all-consumingly enthusiastic or outraged anymore, like I used to be. I find it so easy now to see that a problem can almost always be viewed from many different angles, and consequently I often find myself feeling ambivalent.

In this mood, I came across among my papers a few lines from student days:

Come to me and comfort me for what life has become
Smooth away the fatigue from my eyelids
and all my double-mindedness
Lay your hand upon my gut
and let the day's brood of trouble
be delivered in tears

Thus already back then, already a yearning for someone to comfort me—but even then just as now, I realize, an equal need to be left alone. Already then plagued by ambivalence, by the knowledge that it is seldom details we need comfort for, but life in its entirety.

The Prophet of Comfort, Second Isaiah, speaks to me. "Remember these things, O Jacob, and Israel, for you are my servant." Almost twenty times he repeats that double name. Nothing makes me feel so safe, for in this he speaks of me.

The ford of the Jabbok, and Jacob has been away a long time; he has given good cause for his name "Betrayer," which is what "Jacob" means. He has cheated his twin brother out of the inheritance and the blessing, lied to his dying father, and enriched himself at his father-in-law's expense. It is clearly no saint who is now en route home to meet his brother and possibly seek forgiveness. There is now nothing left separating him from his destination but a little brook, and Jacob is afraid; afraid, but cunning still. He hopes to bribe his brother by sending on ahead his possessions, his livestock, his wives and children.

He himself is left alone to wrestle with the angel. Some of us recognize well enough this combat and the twisted body that results from it, the mark of God that we bear from that moment on. God's angel gives Jacob a blow on the hip and a new name, Israel. The name means that he has fought with God, but also that he fights for God. He gets a double name.

His people also may inherit that double name, and I, too, want to inherit it. When I hear God say, "You, Lena, you are a betrayer *and* a warrior for God"—then I know that God sees me. All my history, all my dividedness. It makes me feel very secure.

For my part, I can't always see even where the boundary runs between the one and the other; the twins Jacob and Israel do not lie within me as if in one and the same womb, each with his own umbilical cord, easy to distinguish when they emerge into the light. They are not like the halves of a brain or a walnut. Instead they are entwined around each other, interwoven with one another like a lace or simply like one big tangled mess, almost impossible to unravel.

Sometimes the name is even tripled. "But now hear, O Jacob my servant, Israel whom I have chosen! Thus says the LORD who made you, who formed you in the womb and will help you: Do not fear, O Jacob my servant, Jeshurun whom I have chosen." The third name, Jeshurun, is one we don't really know the meaning of. But it is something along these lines: upright, honest, genuine, firm. It sounds like a promise. Someday, somewhere, that will be my identity. Not Jacob and Israel, but Jeshurun. Then the dividedness will be overcome, then I will be genuine, then I shall have only one name.

And I am in a better situation than Jacob was when I wrestle with God, when the angel confronts me in the night. Jacob was not permitted to know the angel's name, yet he doubtless understood with whom he was struggling. But I, when I throw myself on the bed and cry—I truly do know his name! He is no longer unknown. I know who he is. It is of him that Pilate said, "Behold the man!" He stands there smitten over the back with scourges, beaten about the head, wearing the insignia of mockery, a crown of thorns and a red mantel. And Pilate says, "Behold, the man!" Yes, and I behold my God.

And perhaps the question itself takes on a different tone when I realize who it is I'm asking. It is to the crucified One that I say, "Why must I have pain like this every day?" He knows how it feels to be spat on in the face, when I ask whether he can understand anything so disgusting or wish it to happen. If I have taken a beating, I can talk with one who was also bloodied and bruised. When I cry out that I am alone and have no one to help me, I am crying out to him who was seized in Gethsemane. Then, truly, for me the question itself takes on a whole new character.

The Whole Heart

Matt 22:37; Deut 6:5; 1 Sam 7:3; Ps 86:12; Jer 24:7; Matt 5:8; Ps 51:12; Mark 7:24–30; Luke 7:1–10; Mark 9:14–29; Ps 130

If this dividedness lies so deep within us, what do we do about all those many sayings in the Bible about being whole-hearted? I would like to know! Is there such a thing after all as whole-hearted faith? Did Jesus ever encounter it? What does he say himself?

One day, the Pharisees press him on the issue of which commandment is the greatest and first commandment. He answers, as he surely learned to do when he was a little boy: "You shall love the Lord your God with all your heart, and with all your soul, and with all your strength."

All your heart, all your soul, all your strength—this is a tough commandment for us inconsistent wafflers. And the Old Testament sounds the same theme in various ways and in many places. As an exhortation: "Keep yourselves with a whole heart to the Lord; worship him, and no other!" Or as an intention: "I give thanks to you, O Lord my God, with my whole heart!" The prophet casts it in the form of a demand: "They shall be my people and I will be their God, for they shall return to me with their whole heart."

It doesn't get any simpler with the pure heart. "Blessed are the pure in heart, for they will see God," says the Master. "Pure" here does not mean guiltless or innocent, but unmixed, as in "pure gold"—and thus the same thing as "whole-hearted." Fortunately the Psalms imply that it's God's business, not mine, to make me pure-hearted: "Create in me a clean heart, O God." That's a prayer I can easily join in with—rather whole-heartedly.

Indeed. But is there something more going on here? Someone has suggested that perhaps we are whole-hearted when we pray for our children, especially if one of them is sick. Jesus found himself in situations such as this, and he responded to the petitioners in varying ways.

On one occasion Jesus has withdrawn himself, but is interrupted. I know how I would have dealt with the situation; I'd have experienced mounting irritation at never being left alone, never getting any real rest. It looks as if he had a similar reaction. A Canaanite woman meets him, crying that he come and help her daughter, who is gravely ill. And he doesn't answer her at all! It seems as if he and those with him will merely pass her by. The disciples clearly sense the awkwardness and draw his attention to the situation. He merely replies that his mission is limited to the people of Israel.

The woman continues her cries and Jesus continues to be completely unpleasant. It's not right to take bread from the children and throw it to the dogs, he says. Doubtless the woman is upset and offended that he would label the pagans as dogs, but her child means more to her than her dignity and she observes slyly that the dogs merely eat the crumbs from the children's table.

Now it is as if Jesus truly sees her for the first time, and he stops. He has been changed. Perhaps he's gained an insight that touches him at heart, that his calling was greater than he previously thought, so that the woman has helped him to see his duty more clearly. He tells the woman that her faith is great and that she shall have what she asks for—her daughter will be healed.

Then there is the son (or servant-boy) of the Roman officer. Here is a man who has power and who knows that Jesus also has power, a power greater than his. He is also a man who knows his place: "I am not worthy to have you come under my roof. But only speak the word, and let the boy be healed." This man, too, is a surprise for Jesus, as well as a cause for joy: "Not even in Israel have I found such faith!" And the boy is healed.

Another difficult and embarrassing situation arises as Jesus comes down from the Mount of Transfiguration. A man with an epileptic boy has begged that the disciples who remained behind would heal the child. But they have not been successful at all, even though the boy's dad has given a very detailed description of the ailment's misery. "Oh how tired I am of your lack of faith! Bring the lad here!" The father comes again with his prayer: "Help us if you can!"—"If I can!" Jesus replies. "All things can be done for the one who believes." The father, as divided within himself as we are, yet undivided in his love for the child, provides for us the word of deliverance: "I believe! Help my unbelief!" It is a prayer the Lord accepts, and this child too is made well.

What sort of faith is this we see here? What is great about it? Is it the stubbornness that we also encounter from others who pray for his help? Is it the notion that Jesus can help, that now there actually is someone who can? What is it that he himself is longing to see in us? It doesn't seem to be the behavior of the disciples that time on the mountain at least! That was a very fragile faith, perhaps nothing but faith in themselves. But the father, who acknowledges his dilemma and turns his double-mindedness over to Jesus, appears to do something right.

Apparently it matters whom we pray to. Faith is above all a matter of direction, of knowing where to turn one's cry. We need not strain ourselves or wait until it feels right, till we are perfect, whole, and pure; we need only know the direction in which to turn. Of course it can be a good thing to gather our thoughts together sometimes, and to pray calmly and without hurry, and above all to let our prayers be followed by silence, so that God has a chance to answer us. But the more important thing is that God is the one we cry out to.

Still, even in our crying out, even when we try to be quiet in our prayers, other thoughts sneak in. I need to buy milk! My back hurts so much! I should phone my colleague! I simply cannot sit down in peace and quiet with a prayer list when the kitchen looks like this! In such situations, I think of Eric Grönlund, a pastor and a leader in Sweden's Christian high school fellowship movement, and of the answer he gave. The question was, "May we smoke when we pray?" "No," said Eric, "but we can pray while we are smoking." Comforting advice! So I start in on doing the dishes or picking up the house, and I give vent to all my worries, and turn to God.

As I pray, I often think about how I used to shoot with a little bow and arrow I made myself when I was about ten years old or so. I wasn't very strong, and the bow wasn't very big. But the arrow was straight and I was obstinately stubborn. It is like that with prayer. It has nothing to do with the strength of an arm or the power of a bow; it depends entirely on the direction of the arrow. Maybe it lands in a far-off mud hole or deep in a swamp. Maybe it drops at our feet, which then stare at it in blank surprise. It doesn't matter, for angels come and pick up these arrows and carry them off in the right direction, along the way between us and him.

We have no need to depend upon ourselves. There is one who wants us to call to him for help, one to long for, more than watchmen long for the morning, more than watchmen for the morning. To cast our prayer and longing toward God, or into the empty void where we hope God possibly might be, that is faith.

A Child Such as This

Amos 2:6; Rom 3:23; Mark 9:36; Mark 10:14; Matt 18:3; Mark 9:42; Matt 18:10; Luke 2:34–35; Luke 11:13; Ps 104:30

All questions assume their extreme significance when they have to do with children. Evil seems its worst in such cases, and not just *seems*—so many children are truly at grave risk. Most of the world's poor are women and the children of poor women; it is here that the great mortality among children occurs. In refugee camps, it is the children who die first. Prostitution can never be justified, and when it involves children it becomes unbearable. But poverty-stricken parents must sometimes sell one of their children for a pittance, just so the rest of the family can survive. Amos describes Israel's offence: "They sell the righteous for silver, and the needy for a pair of shoes." But today the buyer has the greatest guilt, no doubt about it—together with us, who have given the parents no alternative.

The suffering of children also challenges our theories. Every theory should be tested with children, and likewise every theological system. Suffering is punishment, we say perhaps—but what have the little girls of Thailand done? Or: something good always comes out of suffering—but what good comes of refugee children starving to death or of children and families being bombed?

Sometimes our own experience may be that good can result from suffering, gradually and secondarily, but that scarcely is the case with the suffering of children. In fact, nothing should be said about the meaning of suffering that cannot be said in front of children who cower under carpet bombing, or in the cancer ward of a children's clinic, or in a bordello.

Perhaps we say with Paul that "all have sinned and fall short of the glory of God,"—but then we are really talking about adults, aren't we? We don't say this regarding a tiny, tiny child lying in an incubator. He weighs scarcely a few ounces—but his will is strong and he draws his breath in light, quick rhythm, like a little bird, and the glory of God shines through him more strongly than through any "earthen vessel," even an apostle.

Those who need some sort of inherited, collective guilt for their theory of atonement will have to define sin differently from the way I do: I define it as what divides us from God. What can a child such as this have done or what could possibly separate it from God? Is it not in God's hand, whether it lives or dies? The answer is obvious to me. Our primary relationship with God is not defined by the fact that we are forgiven, not even by the fact that we are baptized, but by the fact that we are alive.

Likewise every element of the Christian view of humanity must include children, if for no other reason than that they are most important to the Master himself. Jesus is incredibly solicitous about children; he completely identifies himself with them. He places a child before the twelve, hugs it and says, "Whoever receives one such child in my name receives me." He is angered when the disciples turn away people who come with their babies: "Let the children come to me, do not hinder them; for to such belongs the kingdom of God." Once more the disciples ask, "Who is the greatest in the kingdom of heaven?" And he puts a child in the midst of them: "Truly, I say to you, unless you turn and become like children, you will never enter the kingdom of heaven."

But if he is so concerned about the children, why then does he do so little in their defense? His neglect does not seem especially in line with God's priorities. Children can be hurt so easily. Jesus says, "Whoever causes one of these little ones who believe in me to sin, it would be better for him if a great millstone were hung round his neck and he were thrown into the sea."—"See that you do not despise one of these little ones; for I tell you that in heaven their angels always behold the face of my Father who is in heaven."

But I want something more than mere threats of coming judgment; I want something visible, something now.

God is invisible. It's such a trivial statement that we seldom trouble ourselves to think more deeply about it. God and God's acts are in many ways hidden from us. We have been allowed to know what God is like, what God wants with us, because the only-born son has shown it to us. We know very little about God's glory in heaven, about what eternity, holiness, and blessedness look like, other than vague impressions. Clearly that's not the same thing as knowing what they mean. And this is apparently how it's meant to be.

Jesus of Nazareth was not all that transparent either. It was not obvious to anyone that God was in him, not even to his own mamma. When he was only seven weeks old, she was warned by the aged Simeon: "This child is set for the fall and rising of many and for a sign that is spoken against. Indeed, a sword will pierce through your own soul also." Even *she* was forced to believe; even *she* could not see, could not easily discern who he really was.

The divine was hidden in the earthly and that is how it continued to be. God's promise of an eternal covenant is hidden in the waters of baptism, his nearness, forgiveness, and cure is hidden in the bread and the wine. The truth about Jesus' person and deeds is hidden in the four portraits that the evangelists give us; God's will for his people Israel is sometimes hidden in stories of war and violence. Now, here on earth, God acts invisibly together with human beings; some of these coworkers of God are aware of it and some are not. If a work promises to rescue people or set them free, we can be assured that God is there in it, whether the church is or not.

So we are part of a work in progress, where God's hands are in it along with our own. But surely we could wish that God would want to be more heavy-fisted now and then, that he would prevent people from making the choices they do, that he would put a stop to evil behavior. Yet sometimes God is also helpless. God chooses to be helpless. Genuine love cannot compel the beloved. God cannot force people to be good. We were talking about this once in a confirmation class. "I wish God could at least force presidents to do his will," said a girl. Who doesn't echo her sentiments?

Well, then, what more can we do than to continue, together with God, in all this slow, invisible work to make things better for the children, to make it so that all children can have a good life? We can, of course, protest, cry out, and pray, as always—persistently, as if every child were our own. And perhaps we can pay attention to the other thing he said, that thing about us.

What does it mean to become like a little child? To be guiltless and innocent? The only guiltlessness we adults can attain is the guiltlessness we have in forgiveness, that is, our daily conversion, which is what it means to live in our baptism. This is certainly a good thing, but is there possibly something more?

Can being childlike imply having confidence, trust? But that's something we cannot produce on our own; it may result from a safe, secure childhood, or it may not. Trust in God among adults, whether they grew up feeling secure about themselves or not, is the work of the Spirit; yet merely saying that is to deny personal responsibility.

Being childlike is also a matter of willingness to change and to grow. In fact in antiquity, in Jesus' day, the dominating perspective was that a child was expected to *become* something, not that it *already was* something; a child was expected to grow and become a human being. For the courage to grow and change, we also need the Spirit, which God gladly gives us: "If you then, who are evil, know how to give good gifts to your children, how much more will the heavenly Father give the Holy Spirit to those who ask him!"

It is important to see the connection between change and God's Spirit, who renews the face of the ground every spring, who directs the times and seasons like the winds of heaven. The Spirit can renew and change anxious old biddies and gruff old duffers no less than he can change young men and women cocksure of themselves. We can have nothing to do with God's Spirit if we are not ready for change, renewal, and growth. If we do not want that, if we dare not submit to it, then it is meaningless to pray to the Spirit. Thus, in the end the question is about what we really dare to do and to be.

We Have to Take What Life Gives Us

2 Cor 5:18–29; Isa 6:5

"We have to take what life gives us." That's what she said. I don't remember her name. I do recall that before I made the visit to her home, I got some anxious advice from co-workers, warning me that she was severely afflicted. I also remember her broad back that looked so strong as she bent down to take the cake from the oven. But that was clearly not the case, for she put her hand on her behind as she straightened herself up again, and gave me, as she did so, something between a smile and a grimace.

And so it turned out as it sometimes does—the young pastor ended up receiving wisdom instead of giving it. The lesson for the day: there are certain conditions that are simply given, and we must accommodate ourselves to them. We cannot choose our parents, our social backgrounds, our bodies, or our native talents. There are also certain things that happen to us, things that shape life, our own lives, things that place a framework, boundaries, around what can be done with our lives.

So as I left her, I realized that there is no point in eating our hearts out because we weren't blessed with curly hair and a singing voice, or because we gradually found ourselves in love with the wrong person, or afflicted with chronic pain. Complaining about it only robs us of our strength. We have received something else instead, and if we believe that we are created beings and have a God who helps us with every difficulty, then with some willingness to ask questions and a little gratitude we find ourselves able to cope with those other things.

Asking questions makes good sense, of course. But gratitude? How much can I really say that today I accepted my life for what it is? I wonder if Paul didn't also think about this as he wrote in his second letter to Corinth: "God has reconciled us to himself through Christ, and has given us the ministry of reconciliation; that is, in Christ God was reconciling the world to himself, not counting their trespasses against them, and entrusting the message of reconciliation to us. So we are ambassadors for Christ, since God is making his appeal through us; we entreat you on behalf of Christ, be reconciled to God!"

Weighty words! Paul has a commission, clearly, to announce reconciliation between two parties. Something was definitely wrong between these two—but the two parties are not (as we were required to learn in that confusing classical doctrine of atonement) a wrathful heavenly God and the Son, whose bloody death God took in kind and thereby relented in his wrath. It has to do instead with other broken relationships; there was something that wasn't right between God and *humanity*. And reconciliation is the only path to resolution that Paul has to show us.

It wasn't God's fault. God did not want it to be like this. Human beings rejected God, in many different ways, and became trapped in the web of evil. We were created to be God's friends and beloved possession, but we revolted—all of us did when we made the wrong choice and then perhaps, like Adam, followed it up by dodging the blame.

But nearness can be restored. God, angry over sin and sorry over having been abandoned, came as near to us as God could do. This God, the God of creation, actually became a human being. If we read the underlying Greek text, we see that Paul literally puts it this way: "God was in Christ, reconciling the world to himself." The initiative for this restored nearness was God's own, and it was God who acted in Jesus. The possibility of setting us free was created through obedience—not ours, but the obedience of him who went up to Jerusalem that Passover week. How this can be, I cannot imagine. There is no logical rationale that can account for it. I can only say that if God chose to do it, then it must have been necessary. Otherwise no one would have elected to do anything so horrifyingly desperate—not even God, whose thoughts we do not understand, but about whose love we know a great deal.

God can create this nearness, but we must respond to it. And how do we do that? We respond by acknowledging that we know how things really are and by praying to be set free from it all. We usually refer to this as confession of sins.

But the point of confessing sins is not that we must daily inventory every stupid thing we've done, every evil thought we've had, or every vicious thing we've said. Doing this is only another way of robbing us of our strength; it merely prolongs our enormous self-fixation, our self-absorption, whether we massage our piety, our misery, or our sin. It amounts to giving over to Satan lots of time we could make better use of.

Luther advises us in the Large Catechism to confess whatever compels us to play a part in the evil of life. It sounds like Isaiah in the temple: "I am a man of unclean lips, and I live among a people of unclean lips." So, perhaps this is what we should say: "God, as you and I both know, I am part of a God-forsaking, perverted culture. I carry it in my blood, as well as in my thoughts. I cannot free myself of it by my own powers. Today, what torments me is this . . ."

Precisely here is the point of salvation; this is the moment we are liberated, when God says, "Right! That is indeed how it is! But I now set you free. By the power of the cross, I tear apart the evil net that holds you fast!" That is where God is reconciled.

Likewise, reconciliation always implies the future. God wants us to live facing forward, as those who are forgiven; there is no other way. Forgiveness and a hopeful faith are like twins; they must be received together. If we do not receive them so, we will find ourselves right back at that disagreeable place we were in before being reconciled.

It also looks as if reconciliation is bi-directional. *We* must forgive *God!* We must lay aside our rebellion; we must reconcile ourselves to the life God has given us. It's a life that has been spoiled in numerous ways, but God has also given us the possibility in life for being drawn near, for joy, love, forgiveness, and for good, hard work. We must accept our life; we only get one, our own. It just doesn't work to come around late in the game and ask for another one. I wonder if anyone of us ever gets this right.

I think about my father's mother. I dare not say too much about her, since I was only twelve when she died. But I still hear her voice, the biting humor in the way she talked: "When it rains oatmeal, the poor man has no spoon," and "If we can't get the one we love, then we have to love the one we get." I can remember how she told of being poor on a soldier's few acres and of children who died. Whenever I like, I can see her crippled hands before me, and recall how she could pay attention to whoever came across her path, grandchild, chimney sweep, or police chief. I can remember her unbending conviction: We do what we must do, whatever it takes.

But on the tiled stove in her house this totally unsentimental woman had a gold-rimmed card decorated with forget-me-nots and printed with the words of the hymn, "Thanks to God for my Redeemer."[9] The winter before I turned six, I stood on a stool and learned that hymn by heart. It told me that life was incomparably grand, much greater and more difficult that I had yet understood—but something I truly wanted to know more of.

The same feeling grips me when I hear Arja Saijonmaa[10] singing Inti-Illimani's "I want to thank life."[11] Somewhere in all of this lies an answer, something that says that life broadens out and can become enormous when we dare to step into the unknown, when we slip away from expectations that everything should be pre-planned and idyllic. Life becomes so small when it is constrained by anxiety and fear for our own hide. But it grows large both from sorrow, pain, and tears, on the one hand, and from the return of springtime and from grandchildren and affections new and old, on the other. I want to thank life, for it has given me so much. I want to live reconciled.

Are You Bitter?

Exod 12:8; Exod 15:22–23; 1 Sam 15:32; Lam 1:4; Luke 22:61; Job 5:2; Isa 38:17; Ezek 11:19–20

Oh, how I'd like to be interviewed on TV, to have some slick reporter stick a mike under my chin and ask those TV questions, questions about terrorists and budget proposals, about soccer scores and new hairstyles. "How do you feel about these things?" And I would answer: "How I feel is no concern of yours, but I can tell you what I think." Today, however, the interviewer's question was different.

"Are you bitter?" I had been only half listening and was actually wondering what on earth had happened to this poor wretch on the screen; he must have seen his whole life destroyed—falsely condemned perhaps, or mistreated for years by the medical establishment, or something worse. But it turned out that a car had driven off the road and plowed into his vegetable garden yesterday. *Yesterday!* And here I thought that bitterness was what a person accumulated over time from great disappointments, worriedly nursing the bitterness until it ate its way inward, corrupting and shriveling the soul.

I can't do anything about how TV interviewers misuse language. But I've begun to think about bitterness, how it starts when people choose the dark and difficult things in their life and memories and create from them an image of themselves as wronged, unfairly treated, cruelly manipulated—and powerless against it all. I'm reminded of a poem by Märta Tikkanen.[12]

I sat beside my mother
and held her hand
as the light faded forever from her eyes.

In that moment I promised her
that I never
would say, as she had:
I wasn't given the chance.

What I will say,
if I must, is this:
I didn't get it done.

There is something here, something about taking responsibility for how we make our choices, about the fact *that* we make our choices, and about not blaming someone else. I have to admit, of course, that it is tremendously difficult to say how much choice others have actually had—not least the women of earlier generations. People are paralyzed both by social conditions and by ideas of powerlessness, as well as by the habit of letting someone else make decisions. Making our own choices needs to be something we especially adopt for our own lives.

We choose—and when we choose, we also reject, as we do for example in choosing something as important as a profession or a partner. When we make such a choice we must also mourn what we reject, so that we can truly leave it behind us. Otherwise, when it crops up again further down the road, we might not be able to resist blaming someone else for it: "It was your fault . . . that we decided not to have children . . . that I became a housewife . . . that I've had to stay so long at a job I'm unhappy in, or in a marriage either gone dead, or become completely and utterly destructive."

I go to the Bible to find something on bitterness and perhaps its remedy. It is there like a taste, like the bitter herbs of Passover. Like the water, the bitter water of Marah, the first rest stop after Israel's rescue through the Reed Sea. There are overtones in these uses of the word that imply it touches not only the tongue but the heart as well.

Bitterness also appears in short, utterly natural reactions in response, for example, to the threat of death: "Surely this is the bitterness of death." Or following a catastrophe: "The roads to Zion mourn, for no one comes to the festivals . . . and her lot is bitter." And similarly: "Then Peter remembered the word of the Lord, how he had said to him, 'Before the cock crows . . .' And he went out and wept bitterly." But sometimes bitterness is a sorrow that takes root inward, an unwillingness to give up a loss or an injustice. None other than Job himself warns us: "Surely vexation kills the fool, and bitter jealousy slays the simple."

I can find nothing to justify ongoing bitterness. Instead, I seem to be at yet another place in life where I must accept things for what they are. If I am the cause of my own troubles, then I must ask forgiveness for it and move on. If life has been hard, then I must pray for healing, and be open to it besides. People do have experiences like these. King Hezekiah fell very sick, but he received a promise from God that he need not die quite yet: "Surely it was for my welfare that I had great bitterness; but you have held back my life from the pit of destruction, for you have cast all my sins behind your back."

I'm not saying that this is a simple matter, or that a solution comes instantly, or that it is always something we can manage alone. Sometimes it takes another person, sometimes God's interference, which is always a possibility. This is what God, through the prophet Ezekiel, promised to those who were deported to Babylon: "I will give them a new heart, and put a new spirit within them; I will remove the heart of stone from their flesh and give them a heart of flesh. . . . Then they shall be my people, and I will be their God."

We are deceived furthermore both by our particularly strong expectation that life ought to be fair, and by the idea that when life isn't fair, there has to be someone we can blame. As if it were necessary that we make sense of the riddle, as if there were a debt to be paid. As if we cannot bear it that anything could be utterly meaningless, and we would prefer it if God were a kind of master controller, making everything operate according to the law of tit for tat. But it isn't the principle of fairness that sustains the world; it is the principle of love and of forgiveness.

Similarly, good things also happen without micro-managed fairness. Who of us is worthy of the love and strength we enjoy? Or of the profound insight that gives meaning and pattern to life, that binds us together in mutual understanding and deep compassion? New love is born like the coming of spring. Little girls show their faces like blossoms of Johnny Jump-ups in April. Those things aren't fair either! They are not a privilege due us. They come to us by grace. Despise not the grace of God!

I remember a couple lines from a poem I can't lay my hands on just now: "So we chew on disappointment and pretend to live. It tastes more like dust than blood, and something we forgot to remember. . . ." It's a taste we all know—and if we think that anyone can live an entire lifetime without experiencing it, we are merely being naïve. No such escape has been promised to us. But the cure is coming, if we will just give God enough time to do it his way. Sometimes we must wait for it, destitute.

> Sometimes laying down our wills
> is the only way to endure
> when our plans break like glass in our hand
> and disappointment cuts deep into what we want and what we do
> Run home in the summer evening with everything that hasn't healed
> the foundation stones are still warm from the sun
> and you can crouch down and rest your back against them
> and let the fragrance of jasmine flow in from everywhere
> and the suppleness of boughs in the wind
> and the song of the thrush in the falling darkness
> and the very serenity of stone and grass and tree
> stills our weeping.

The Birds of the Air

Luke 9:57–58; Luke 9:59–62; Luke 10:38–42; Mark 1:17; Matt 8:14–15; Luke 15:8–10; Luke 12:13–21; Luke 18:18–25

Living in Skåne[13] is wonderful in early spring. Today we drove out to do some bird watching, as we often do. We were looking for larks, and stayed first at Häckeberga Castle. The ice there had just barely begun to break up, and the first goldeneye ducks were diving through the openings in it. Around Svaneholm Castle it was blowing fiercely and only the jackdaws were playing in the upper winds. But just north of there, among the rolling prairie swells, a peewit stood shivering beside an ice-covered puddle. And a bit further on, over a ridge, we spied a lark, hanging under the sky, jubilant. So full of hope!

It was a spring landscape that met him, too, in the weeks before Passover, with sun and wind and the hopeful birds. But he sounds as if he is in a grim mood. Sometimes we just can't manage to take in the beauty around us; our sorrow or our concentration on a difficult task is so great that it blots out everything else. Perhaps that's how it was when a man came to meet him on the road to Jerusalem.

"I will follow you wherever you go," he says. And Jesus replies to him, "Foxes have holes, and birds of the air have nests; but the Son of Man has nowhere to lay his head." Talk about a brush-off! And to a couple others whom he invites to join his group, but who first want to resolve some family affairs, he says: "Let the dead bury their own dead; but as for you, go and proclaim the kingdom of

God. . . . No one who puts a hand to the plow and looks back is fit for the kingdom of God."

Things have turned serious now. He has neither time for nor interest in anything other than the mission. Everything else seems unimportant, mere rubbish. Just one thing is necessary, he says to Martha—though naturally, like us, he still needs to eat and rest. But it's as if he has adopted a severer tone than the one he took a few years ago. In those days he walked along the lakeshore and called out to those in the fishing boats, and it all sounded so bright, so exciting, even fun! "Follow me and I will show you how to catch people."

In those days he had time for going along with them to their own synagogue and time to go home with Peter, where Peter's mother-in-law lies sick with a fever. She gets better—and then what happens? She serves him, says Matthew. But the word for "serve" is related to our word *deacon*, and Matthew implies by it that she gave up living at home and followed him, perhaps as the first female disciple. You have to wonder what Peter would have thought about *that!*

There must have been a lot of talk about Jesus. I think of the women who have always gathered together in their daily work—perhaps doing the laundry or attending at childbirth, perhaps in weaving or embroidery—and talked about other people, helpfully or unhelpfully! I still visualize the old men I used to see sitting on the "'liars' benches" in the fishing villages or at the old-folks' homes, which still existed when I was a young pastor. They would call out to me: "Hey, little girly-priest! Come over here! I got somethin' to tell ya."

Probably there were old men in his day, too, limping over to a bench to sit on, sucking on the stumps of their teeth, spitting—though not spitting tobacco like the ones I knew—and griping. "That Jesus fellow says that God is like a female—and no wonder, considering all the womenfolk he has around him! Says God is like an old biddy who loses a coin and cleans the whole house, terrifying every living thing in it, screaming and hunting around, sweeping and moving furniture and what have you! And when she finds it there's more screaming and fussing, and running off to all the neighbors' houses, insisting on a celebration!" "That's about how it is for God to find us," says another one. "Ehh, is that what he means?" say the others, and they go back to grousing and shaking their heads. "I can't even imagine having a coin to lose in the first place! Been a while since I've even seen such a thing!"

One of these old men knew that Jesus had said it wasn't such a bad idea to be poor. There was something about a grain farmer who had kicked the bucket one night, before he had a chance to enjoy his big new barns. And there was that rich young man who acted so splendid and—truth be told—self-righteous. He got taken down a peg or two, he did! Jesus had told him that he couldn't take a single nickel with him if he wanted to end up in the life to come. This was too much for the fellow, and though the incident didn't do the Master any good, if the rumors are true, he still wouldn't compromise. Strange!

There was also something about how it is just as difficult for a rich person to enter the kingdom of heaven as it is for a camel to get through the eye of a needle. At this they laugh and say, "Oh no! You've got to be kidding!" And they double up in laughter again, until tears run down their cheeks and, no fooling, drool glistens on their beards. And the Master goes on his way, uncompromising.

The Power and the Glory

On two beams
with three spikes
my hell was nailed fast.

This alone gives me strength.
This alone keeps me going.
This alone is why I want to live.

The Power
(1 Cor 1:18)

Eye for Eye, Missile for Missile

John 3:16; John 1:18; Isa 59:14–17; Exod 34:14; Matt 7:1; Amos (esp. ch. 5); Luke 3:9; Matt 11:3; Isa 61:1–2; Isa 35:4–6; Luke 4:16–20; Matt 5:38–39

There is so much violence in the Old Testament. There are so many passages about a God who wants revenge. And many of them, it seems to me, have something primitive about them, something as removed from us as the ancient Icelandic sagas, as alien as the methods of the Mafia.

In the same way, revenge raises its head in the political context, first as "acts of retaliation" in the Middle East, then in the US reaction to the September 11 catastrophe and the carpet-bombing of the people of Afghanistan. Equally among Jews, Muslims, and Christians there are some who insist that their actions are justified in their holy scriptures. I can't speak for the first two, but how does it look from a Christian perspective? Doesn't our Scripture say, in numerous places, "Vengeance is mine, says the Lord"? How should we respond to this?

First of all, we have to be fair and respectful toward the Bible, recognizing that it doesn't say the same things about God throughout, but that its presentations of God vary. The Bible is filled with people who live with God, who believe and doubt, who have longings and hopes, who love and hate—and who have their own ideas about God. Those ideas—just like ours—are more or less skewed.

Perhaps we are right in asking, then, whether there was any point in Jesus' coming? Did it make any difference? Did we learn anything new? Or does God remain cruel and vengeful? According to John, something has radically changed: "God so loved the cosmos[14] that he gave us his only Son."—"No one has ever seen God; it is the only Son, who is close to the Father's heart, who has made him known." Jesus shows us what God is like; he does it through what he says, what he does, what he is. For this reason he corrects all other ideas of God. To be a Christian is to believe that God is just like Jesus Christ.

What about vengeance, then? It is certainly there, especially when the people of Israel desert their God and provoke his jealousy with foreign gods. Or what about when God saw that "justice was turned back, and righteousness stood at a distance; for truth stumbled in the public square"? In response God "put on garments of vengeance for clothing, and wrapped himself in fury as in a mantle." How should we receive a God like this, a God easy to fear and difficult to love? We continue to read the Old Testament, even in worship services. What does it have to do with us?

A God who can be called "jealous" (or "zealous," as some translations have it), a God who tolerates no competition—that God is indeed relevant to us. But a God who sends us both good and evil, that sort of God Jesus repudiates. Jesus likewise repudiates a God who punishes. Evil has its own consequences and comes from another source.

Still, there are two good points to make about the saying, "vengeance is mine." First, we need to lay the emphasis on the word *mine.* If anyone at all is to take vengeance, it is God, not human beings. God reserves that as a personal right, just as much as the right to judge. Jesus underscores this in the Sermon on the Mount: "Do not judge, so that you may not be judged!"—and he provides variations on it in many other places. We confess it ourselves in the Creed: "and he will come again to judge the living and the dead." We should perhaps start taking it seriously.

The second thing to notice is that vengeance and judgment are parallel, or two sides of the same coin, depending on whether we are the perpetrator or the victim. This is especially clear among the prophets, perhaps foremost in Amos. The oppressor will be judged, the oppressed shall be raised up; the one who strikes down shall be condemned, the victim will be set free. This is how God's judgment and vengeance looks.

But even this is not enough for me. I go to Jesus. What he has to say about vengeance, he doesn't actually say; but he implies it. There must have been a discussion of the subject between John the Baptist and Jesus. When John begins preaching, he starts out in traditional prophetic style: "Shape up, good people! God's Messiah is coming soon! It's time to get your act together!" Or like this: "Even now the ax is lying at the root of the tree!" But when Jesus does come, he doesn't judge—he forgives. It looks as if this confuses John, who had staked his whole life on this one thing. From prison, facing death, he asks, "Are you 'the one who is to come,' or are we to wait for another?"

Jesus' answer combines two texts from Isaiah—leaving out, however, the word about vengeance. Perhaps he is saying to John, "You are right—and wrong. I am indeed the Messiah, but the day of judgment does not lie within the bounds of history."

In the synagogue at Nazareth he pursues the same method. He reads from the Isaiah scroll: "The Lord has anointed me; he has sent me to bring good news . . . to proclaim liberty to the captives . . . to proclaim the year of the Lord's favor. . . ."

But he actually does not finish reading the entire sentence; he stops before the words that follow: "and the day of vengeance of our God." He must have had some definite reason for doing so. In addition to all this, we have a record of his own consistent attitude, in that he never retaliates. We can calmly claim that he is opposed to taking vengeance, and that he awaits God's judgment on the oppressor.

And are we also able to deal with his instruction in the Sermon on the Mount? There he says, "If anyone strikes you on the right

cheek, turn the other also." But this is so difficult, so absurdly difficult, in view of acts of terrorism, for example. It is so outrageously
difficult to say this to someone whose husband or partner has
struck her. I find it difficult to believe that a Christian should be expected to endure violence simply because it affects only her. We
have to find some way to fight against violence and evil.

But when it doesn't work to take the path of love—the path
that Jesus instructs us to take—the answer is not that we should
turn immediately to the path of power and revenge. For there is
also a way of order and dignity, one that seeks to bring about re-
forms within the bounds of the law. This is the way of all democ-
racies, the way of peace negotiations and courts of law. It is the way
Paul and Luther trusted in, the way taken by Gandhi and Martin
Luther King Jr.

What do we succeed in solving by this means, whether at
home, in the workplace, at school, in the political realm?

When must we resort to force, to armed force? Absolutely as a
last resort! There are some occasions when it may well still be necessary, given the state of the world.

But every option must be tried, tested with a "conscience en-
lightened by the Word of God"—as I used to hear it put among
the devout in the 1950s. The whole while we must keep in mind
that Jesus himself trod only the way of love. That was how he over-
came his foes—but it cost him his life. How then must we conduct
ourselves?

Barbed Wire and Thorns

Exod 7:14–11:10; 2 Sam 17:40–50; Eph 6:10–18

The six-year-old is watching a video with her older brothers: *Moses, Prince of Egypt*. From time to time she becomes fiercely indignant.

"Is God allowed to do this?"

"Go ask Grandma," says her mother. And I begin a long and tortuous explanation, which will have to do until we see each other again.

"No, God isn't allowed to do this. It wasn't God who did it. It was the Enemy. They were the ones who had it wrong. But Jesus has told us how God really is. . . ."

"Okay, I see," she says, and slouches down on the sofa again, traveling with her stuffed animals back to an imaginary rain forest in her imaginary Land of Tropica.

Dismissed! *Me!* The one who has traveled around and spoken on this topic and believed that this is one of the most difficult questions to resolve, and one of the most important, if there is ever to be any faith left in our culture. We are, of course, all too aware that darkness and evil exist, both within us and out there in the world at large. And that this darkness neither is God nor comes from God—this we must believe.

It isn't such a blithely simple thing for everyone as it is for this little girl, I know. But I find it hard to rightly understand why, since I have never thought that everything in the Bible applies in the same degree, or is equally "true," or that we must believe it all in the same way. For in fact it isn't the book that comes first, but God. Once we begin to believe in God, or merely become interested in God, we can go to the Bible to learn more. But the Bible is not something so simple as a book about God; it is rather a book about people who live together with God and about their testimony to what that is like.

The very expression "Word of God" as applied to the Bible is foreign to the Bible itself. When the Bible speaks of "God's Word," it is referring to God's creative or re-creative word, or the word that calls a prophet or some other person. But above all it is the incarnated Word, the person of Jesus Christ, who in a new and sometimes unexpected way shows us what God is like. It is not a book that must be rigidly believed in all its parts, so that for the book's sake we must adopt every era's ideas of God. It is God we believe in first; then we go to the book to learn more about what it means to be human when there is a God who lives and who is the Father of Jesus Christ.

It is awful that our children are so continually taught the old stories of a God who resorts to violence. Surely they have enough violence in their lives already, whether fiction or reality. In our house we have done away with some of it, but of course not every one has access to a theological grandma.

"Grandma, I think I get Jonah and Noah mixed up. Do you think they will be angry?"

Grandma thinks they might be. Both of these guys tended to get a little huffy.

"Well, I don't really care!" says the child. "Besides, I think the fish shoulda swallowed Noah, too, 'cuz he let all those others get drownded."

And then we have David and Goliath. The text about them is to be read in church this week, and the story boasts that God does not conquer with the sword—as if a stone in a sling were less violent! What are we to do with a text like this? Or take Paul's image of God's warrior—must we have images of war at all, when we see how frightfully abhorrent war really is?

The other difficult and important question I think we must deal with, if faith is not to die out, concerns the idea that religion is something private. It most certainly is not. For one thing, a Christian lives more or less within a community that worships God together. But above all we believe that God works in history, especially through the historical person of Jesus from Nazareth. Yet God also works by dealing with and speaking to a few others of us—who certainly hear wrongly at times. We call God the God of history, to which those who are most conservative or world-rejecting nod their assent. But history in process is called politics, as for instance in trade policies or policies on refugees.

It wasn't all that long ago that the Second World War was current history, history in the making, and Christians had to decide whether to be politically involved or not. I am reading about the Holocaust in a book titled *Tell Your Children of It*,[15] and again I am filled with horror, nauseated by shame and disgust. I weep for children who died before I was born. One child, then another and another—it is easy to be moved to tears when one sees pictures of their faces. But a million and a half children—can I take it in? Can I even begin to imagine it?

There is one thing I believe I am beginning to understand: "One post-war myth is that refusal to maintain order in the extermination camp or to take part in mass shootings was punished with death. We know, however, of no such cases" (p. 46). "The

Holocaust took place ultimately because, at the most fundamental level, people killed other people in large numbers over an extended period of time" (p. 54). It had nothing to do with some sort of evil machinery; it had to do with people.

Can people do whatever they like? Are all of us subject to such possibilities? Someone once asked me, "What would you have done, if you had been a passenger on the *Estonia?*"[16] I like to think that in such a situation I would have stayed with the children who were left behind to die. But would I really have done it? I don't know. It is easy enough to sense hell's presence in the gas chambers, or in the furnaces, or in the water, but I also sense equally in the depth of my own soul.

Once I was showing my confirmation students the church vestments, in order to explain the liturgical colors. On the lilac-colored chasuble, worn by the pastor for Lenten worship, there was an embroidered cross of thorns over the entire back. I asked what it was and what it had to do with Lent and suffering.

"It's barbed wire," said a boy, "for the sake of all prison camps."

I didn't correct him. Why should I? Perhaps there was barbed wire from Auschwitz in the Savior's crown.

Growing along the Ground

Ps 25

There are two trees up here in Nordingrå,[17] and these two trees are a lot like me. Or maybe it's the other way around. The maple, near the corner of the cowshed, has several trunks. When the wind picks up, it creaks and screeches; the sound makes it easy to see why people used to believe in trolls and forest she-demons.

I do the same thing. When the wind takes my hair and blows it every which way, I shriek and screech, complaining to God and anyone else who'll listen. God tolerates it better. God tolerates it quite well! In fact, it's how the two of us stay in touch in stormy times: I complain and God puts up with it.

The other tree is a pine, out beside the water at Norrfälls Bay. It's not just twisted; it actually has three or four major kinks. It stands there in direct opposition to the wind off the sea, which bends it down against the stony ground. But then it rights itself again. And each year it bears new little green cones. One of the first things I do when we come here each summer is to go out and greet that pine tree, to see how she survived the winter. And there she is. She has a secret: Grow for a while along the ground if you can't stand up straight just now.

Crooked trees truly have their own beauty. I pat her scaly bark and say, "Hang in there, sister!" I lie down next to her for a bit, on a bench set up beside the plank walkway that stretches over a field of rounded stones, millions of stones, long ago washed smooth by the sea and now abandoned by it, exposed to wind and sky. Light and shadow coming through the branches of the pine fall upon my face, and my soul begins to be at peace.

Sometimes the clear June light rises white against the night sky for a brief moment, and then withdraws like a breath exhaled. The air is cool, the wind off the bay comes almost straight out of the east against the red and gray rocks, and I clamber over them. I may not leap from one to another, like the grandchildren do, but just as neatly I climb down to the water's edge and carefully wade out a little. Careful as I try to be, I still scare the scoters; they run clumsily across the surface of the water before lifting off. The gulls are more blasé and simply move a little further out on the bay. A tern dives, as slender and precise as a classically schooled ballerina.

Sometimes there is fog, too, coming in from the sea in chunks, like weariness. We have to drive the car through it very slowly, so as not to run off the edge of the road when it turns sharply on a downhill grade. Otherwise we have to get out and walk, damp and cold, breathing heavily. It's like every weary day that takes a deliberate exercise of the will just to make it through, hour by hour. Just to reason with a body that does not want to climb another stair or to put on anything that isn't very soft. Just to coax a poor old head that only wants to read detective novels. To muster self-discipline just to brush one's teeth.

But on the days when mere piano music pelts me like buckshot in my aching muscles, when I seem to have completely forgotten the art of sleeping, when sensitivity has been intensified in every nerve ending, then there is no question of coaxing myself to do anything. On those days, I simply have to ride it out.

Of course, this too can be done: getting through the business of doing nothing. Occasionally in times like this, I notice that someone is sitting beside me, someone who knows everything there is to know about weakness, about having no strength. Sometimes he probably has other things to do; he has to take care of the whole wide world, after all, and so I too will get by. Perhaps this is what it means to grow along the ground.

To Be in Pain

It would be nice to be green, of course. Green would be quite helpful. An angry green everywhere it hurts. So that it would stab people in the eye, so that no one could smile politely and say, "Oh surely not you! You always look so fresh!" Actually, though, green is the wrong color. Pain isn't green like moss or dandelion leaves, or like a lilac bush or the eyes of a forest sprite[18] or her fir-bough skirt.

Pain is red, like a knife in the flesh, like blood that swims before your eyes, that oozes out between the legs. Like a whack on the back of the neck that drives you to your knees, like a cramp in the gut so bad you want to vomit.

Or pain is ice blue, cold as the winter wind or cramps in the calves of your legs, tingling in your hands and feet, like a storm of hailstones, making its way up your arms and turning your elbows stiff. It's like a screen thrust through the middle of your head, so that half of you is distant, frozen, detached, and the pulse in your temple thuds far, far off.

Most of all pain is gray, gray and heavy like an elephant skin of fatigue flung over you, weighing you down to the ground. Like muscles of clay, or slime in your brain, and irritation in thick folds over your back.

The truth is, however, that you really can't describe pain. There are no words for it. For while you're in the midst of it, your mind is too muddled to find words, or to invent them when there aren't any. When it overwhelms you, like deep water or darkness or fire, or like when your brother pushes you down the nettle-infested hill behind the outhouse, you simply do not have enough energy for it. And you cannot relive pain; you can't summon it back to analyze it, label it, pull it apart, and make it manageable.

Can you describe what living with pain is like at all, especially to someone who doesn't suffer it, to someone who is unaware of her body's willing and easy movements? In simple propositions? Perhaps. You wake up stiff as a post. Your feet are like strange objects, your hands clumsy as boxing gloves. You wish you had a handrail from the bed to the toilet and then to the coffee maker. You have to take your coffee in bed, and you need a washable bedside rug because you spill the coffee on it. You fall over chairs, knock over vases, stumble over thresholds; you lose your grip on the dog's leash. You're shocked at your posture reflected in the hall mirror; you take the mirror down.

You put on a little weight. Candy elevates the blood sugar and briefly dampens the pain. Besides, cocoa brings good luck, as even scientists recognize. I am a chocolate person, and I now have a bit of a tummy.

The world shrinks; small concerns become big issues. You can't lift your arm to hang up a winter coat or to screw in a light bulb. You need sweaters that button up the front; pullovers won't do. You need your own pillow and your own naptime at midday. You don't really have the energy to keep explaining it to everyone. You are less inclined to travel; anyway it hurts even to ride the train.

You have less money. You can't prepare a proper and thrifty lunch, so you live on coffee and sandwiches. You pull yourself together in order to tidy up the kitchen, and then you spend the entire next day in bed. You stagger between the times when the pain is at its worst and so you take pills by the handfuls, and the other times when the pill-induced fog in your head is thickest and so you take as few pills as possible, and instead swear at your knees and shoulders. Better angry than depressed, as they say in the women's movement.

You become irritable. You cannot tolerate strong light and loud noises. If you live with teenagers, both you and the kids are in for it. You can't endure long meetings or pointless arguments; you couldn't before either, but then you could hide it. You prefer not to shake people's hands, since the pain it brings is like a bolt of lightning. But can you bear to explain it to people even one more time? Or is it better just to accept getting a reputation for being snooty? Maybe the simplest thing is to put on a bandage and let people tell *you* about the time they sprained *their* hand. It makes sense; it does the job. Anyone can easily identify.

Every now and then someone asks me, "Have you learned to live with the pain?" NO! I usually say. Not so that I can stop it or lessen it or make it more comfortable. Not so that I can welcome it back on its return visits with a good-natured "Aha! So it's you again, you little devil!" Not so that, after all these years, I have learned to write it into the calendar in order to make sure there is just enough time set aside for other things, too. Instead, I greet it with rage, defiance, and cursing—and I'm glad I can!

Other times I have brooded over whose fault it is. If only I hadn't rebelled against being raised as a girl, or taken "the pill," or gone barefoot in the grass, or worn red dresses—one explanation is as good as another. I've heard them all—except the last, which I made up myself just to end the conversation!

People have given me plenty of suggestions. If they cannot or do not want to do anything else for me, but reluctantly acknowledge that I have as much pain as I say I have, and not as little pain as my critics say I have, or appear to have (are you following me?) or should have, considering my work schedule or my stage of life or the fact that I still seem to accomplish things competently—then the explanations come.

Perhaps fibromyalgia[19] is a result of a faulty balance of acid and base, or sleep disturbances (or the reverse), over-exertion, ambitions, laziness, shortage of silicon, sadness, viral infection, inattention, beautiful weather and long summers—you name it (the last two I made up myself, and for the same reasons as for the "red dress"!).

And then good advice: the two most common are, "Have you tried a vegetarian diet?" and "Have you surrendered yourself to Jesus?" Somewhere in all this it feels like being attacked, naturally. Just as it is the patient, and not the nurse, who knows when the pain returns, we need to respect the one who lives with the pain and trust that she has done what she can. Those who really want to help her can ask, "Is there anything I can do for you?" And they should not take offense if they are not asked for the deep, supportive conversation they dreamed of providing, but are asked instead to do the vacuuming, to go buy milk, or to mind the phone, or something equally unexciting.

There is sorrow, of course, especially during the first year, when you grieve over your lost health. When what is taken from me is something tightly woven into my very being, my identity, then life seems hardly worth living. When a child dies, when a beloved one leaves, when I can no longer work, all that's left then is emptiness, ashes, a messy, foul-smelling beach at low tide.

Yet, often the lust for life returns in small things. Very thin threads hold us together in our greatest need, a certain strain of music, sighing in the trees, another person's gentle touch, an old prayer. And suddenly one day I *see* the dog chasing its tail. Coffee tastes good again. I have to go get my hair cut. Someone asks to meet me, and it doesn't seem like a burden, but an opportunity.

Like Clay in His Hand

Jer 1:4–6; Jer 2:13; Isa 55:1; John 7:37–38; Rev 21:6; Jer 20:7–9; Jer 18:1–6; 1 Cor 4:1–2; 2 Cor 4:4–6; Eph 1:9–10; 1 Kgs 19:11–13; Matt 6:28–29

When I turned seventeen, my mother gave me a hymnal; inside she'd written in the words of a hymn, one of the annoyingly motivational sort. It didn't do any harm, though, partly because I was strong and partly because at that age, we are capable of unbounded laziness. But now the third verse rings in my head. "Work for the night is coming. You who go out early, do you throw down your tools? Do you think your work is done?"[20] No, I don't think my work is done! I've only had to exchange tools—and not just my old Smith-Corona for a Mac. I've also been forced to find new ways of doing things, since the pain has made it difficult for me to endure the long days of congregational work.

I was sixteen when I was called. It's nothing to brag about when I compare my situation with Jeremiah's, but there is a lot in his story that I feel I understand. He was called when he was still a fetus in the womb of his mother, herself a nameless wife of a priest. Early on he heard God's voice, and he raised objections: "I am too young!"

Yet he goes. He saw as well as I do how much there needs to be done in a nation, a culture, a world, where people pass by the well of fresh water, the living water that God gives freely, where they prefer instead water sitting in cisterns—like the water they nowadays prefer poured into bottles and carbonated!

It isn't easy to live out the call of trying to talk about what God wants. In a Danish children's Bible I come across these lines about the prophet Elijah: "He was called and consecrated to be a lonely man, one who could expect to have no private happiness in life, who would stand alone against kings, live alone in the desert, always a beggar, always a refugee. God would constantly be with him, of course. But that's just it with the business of 'waiting on God,' as it's called: we cannot decide ourselves when God should speak and when he should have a use for us. We can't expect God to show up at an appointed time, and we have no assurance that God will speak to us when we ourselves need to hear his voice."

Whether prophet or ordinary parish pastor—for most of us there are times when we want to leave it all behind, when we think we just can't take it anymore. "Then within me there is something like a burning fire shut up in my bones; I am weary with holding it in, and I cannot," says Jeremiah, and he gives in, for he has no other choice.

Were you, too, doubled over in pain, Jeremiah, and did you weep and weep, when you said to God, "O Lord, you have enticed me, and I have let myself be enticed." And what did you think, when God took you to the potter's house? The two of you found him working at his potter's wheel, and sometimes he made a mess of things with the clay. Then he made it into a new vessel, as he desired to make it, and God said to you, "Can I not do with you just as this potter has done? Just like the clay in the potter's hand, so are you in my hand." I do believe in the potter's possibilities for making even a "night jar" of me. Precisely because I have become useless, chipped and broken, he neither mends nor repairs. Instead he roughly squeezes the old clay together again and starts over.

Paul also speaks of jars in connection with his calling. It's not in his first letter to Corinth, where he still has a little distance and wants to be regarded as a servant of Christ and a faithful administrator of God's mysteries. But in the second letter, he takes more the posture of an insider. He writes: "For it is the God who said, 'Let light shine out of darkness,' who has shone in our hearts to give the light of the knowledge of the glory of God in the face of Jesus Christ. But we have this treasure in clay jars, so that it may be made clear that this extraordinary power belongs to God and does not come from us."

The treasure, the mystery that has been entrusted to him, has found a place within the apostle, in his sick, weak body, and without it he is next to nothing. What treasure? What mystery is he talking about? We have it set out for us in the Letter to the Ephesians. "God has made known to us the mystery of his will, according to his good pleasure that he set forth in Christ, as a plan for the fullness of time, to gather up all things in him, things in heaven and things on earth."

Paul has painted it all just a little too beautiful, I think. It is not self-evident that we are transparent just because the material we're made of is fragile. It is not inevitable that glory spreads itself around a sick and afflicted person; more likely it's complaining and bitterness. If there is just a little wine, I've said to myself, let's hope it's good wine and not sour. But often enough, I think, it's just plain vinegar. Still Paul insists that if God speaks through you when you have nothing left to give, then it's obviously God who's doing the speaking! Provided, of course, that God is allowed to speak and you keep your mouth shut!

But what did the people around Paul actually see, the treasure or just the pot? Did they typically see the fellow himself or just his pitiful performance? We know that the reaction wasn't always the same. Probably they were in the habit of looking right past the soul, that tattered old thing, and looking instead for the beautiful, the healthy and strong, the efficient. It's no different today.

The church is not immune from this way of relating to people. So many church workers exhaust themselves with arrogance, find themselves pressured by cell phones, calendars, and the clock; they have no time for the stillness needed for hearing God. I am privileged, I know. I have lots of time to be still; I have a great deal of time when I can't be anything but still.

Yet I too am afflicted, afflicted by the inability to work, by being useless. Yesterday, I didn't do a thing; I just sat it out. Today, though, I answered two letters *and* emptied the recyclable trash *and* spoke nicely on the phone with a young colleague. But there is so much more to do as well: reading, writing, washing, mending, ironing, comforting. . . . What does God want to do with all these broken pots? Has God thought about it at all? Could they be filled with something sensible, something useful perhaps?

I go to bed early and get up late. I dream, and in my dream I find myself in one of Elsa Beskow's pictures[21]; it's not the first time. Tonight the picture is for one of Alice Tegnér's songs:[22]

> *Goosey, Goosey jingle, loan me your wings!*
> *"Whither will you fly?"*
> *Fly to my father's farm.*
> *There it's good to be*
> *where the swallow sings,*
> *where the onion sprouts,*
> *where the cuckoo calls,*
> *where the little child sits,*
> *little girl sits playing*
> *with golden apples, with golden apples.*

Yes! There it is! A typical four-sided farm in Skåne, with thatched roofs and a cobblestone yard. A yellow tulip shoots up in the grass between the stones; the swallow is in the air, the wind blows wherever it wills and the child plays under a blooming cherry tree—or maybe it's a pear tree. But something in the picture has changed. Now there are benches painted green and set against the white walls of the buildings in my dream. And there we are, all God's pots, set up in a row on the benches. And do you know what God the Father has done? He has put lilies in the pots! And "they neither toil nor spin, yet I tell you, even Solomon in all his glory was not clothed like one of these." Can it really be as simple as that?

Meditation on Hoarfrost

Song 2:7; 2 Cor 12:9; 1 Pet 5:8; Rev 12:12; 1 Cor 15:55; Luke 22:35

The morning darkness outside the window is replaced with completely white fog. As it lifts, clear sunlight shines on something I have scarcely ever before seen in Skåne, hoarfrost. It looks just like ice, covering every branch, every blade of grass, every withered leaf. There was in fact a cold rain last evening, soaking everything, and then the temperature fell quite suddenly. It is unbelievably beautiful; I stand transfixed for a good long time.

But it is so fragile. On the southeast, where the sun strikes, the ice melts quickly and soon falls to the ground, faster and faster in a clattering crescendo. I see people, strangers to one another, stopping to look, point and comment. "So fragile," I say to myself, no doubt because I have just been going around meditating on something else that's fragile. That fragile quality in me that affects me like an affliction of doubt—that quality of brittleness we human beings have just where we are most like God: in our capacity for love and our capacity for good, creative work.

This morning, I think to myself, was as fragile as falling in love for the first time, as when a young person is in an uproar and doesn't even know herself, as when inexperience can so easily entice her to proceed too fast and "awaken love before it is ready." Or fragile like an old man's trembling hunger to begin again, to dare to open himself, to entrust himself to another person again, in tenderness, caressing, and desire for sexual intimacy—so easily exposed to ridicule, to devastated loneliness, to new disappointment and old scars.

But shouldn't we be all the stronger precisely here in the matter of love, in this aspect of our God-likeness? Shouldn't we rightly expect that here of all places God would enable us to overcome, that God would provide extra resources to help us avoid disappointment and desertion? Is it that this very divine characteristic is especially difficult for us, or that evil is especially interested in attacking us precisely where we are most like God? I do not know.

It is just the same with work. Truly creative work, the sort requiring that a person expose herself to the very depth of her soul, is all too seldom carried out in full, and even more seldom accepted. Why on any ordinary day am I unable to do what I'd like to do, even when I see that it would be a good thing to do? That letter to someone in sorrow; that extra bit of patience with a wounded child; that bright idea that needs working up into a good sermon. Why are so many worthy things never accomplished because there just isn't enough energy for doing them?

One gets a little touchy about the word "strength" when one doesn't have much of it. Lots of earnest people have reminded me that strength is made perfect in weakness; it's what Paul says, so it must be true. But Paul's words don't mean what people often insist they do, that God promises to give strength whenever one is weak. Not at all. He is talking about persistent weakness and implies that God *can* be especially visible in it.

Another very common form of pious talk runs like this: God gives us the strength we ask for. Well, God doesn't; I can tell you that much! God in no way gives us the strength we think we need, the strength, for example, to prevent our children from going through tough times. It is conceivable that God gives us the strength that *God* thinks we need—but if that were so, God would be party to creating a share of utterly destructive situations, and I simply do not believe it. Thus the question becomes instead one of just how powerless God is with regard to us and with regard to evil.

God has established boundaries for evil, and also for the exercise of his own power. Where do they lie?

Those studying for confirmation class often try to put the pastor into a corner by asking whether God is able to create a rock so large even God cannot lift it. The answer would perhaps be virtually the same one Job got: If you ask a question like that, you only demonstrate how little you really understand about me. But to what degree is God bound by the laws of nature, the inherent functions of his own creation? Sometimes of course it looks as though they are set aside, both now in our own day and when Jesus walked the earth. Such events are what we call miracles, although God does much stranger and more wonderful things, and the rules that get broken are reasonably regarded as God's own. But on the whole, we must still reckon with the fact that the law of gravity applies if a child falls out of a window, whether that child has believing parents who pray for it or not.

And indeed, I am certainly also well aware of the idea that God cannot force a person to do good, that God relinquishes control. Likewise I acknowledge the fact that we sometimes refuse to accept the good that is offered to us. And that the devil goes around like a roaring lion because he knows that the time he has left is short. But good God! Couldn't you at least provide some extra resources when I want to be loving or to do my work, when I want so badly for things to go well?

Evil, too, has its boundaries; for example, it cannot create anything new, but can only tear down. Love can fall apart; trust can be destroyed; forest and savannah can be turned to desert. I also believe and sometimes think I actually see that evil just doesn't understand real, sacrificial love. When we cease thinking about ourselves, when we are wholly intent on helping someone else, that in itself can break the vicious cycle and strike the weapon from the hands of evil. And in the end evil is its own end. When the last enemy comes, that last thing Satan has at his disposal, namely death, then also evil's time is done. Once death reaches us, we are thereafter beyond the reach of everything and everyone else, except God.

. But this doesn't solve the question of how we are to deal with a broken love or with powerlessness all those times when we don't have what it takes. Yet I sometimes wonder whether we finally come to the same point as the disciples did, when Jesus sends them out again after his resurrection. "That previous time, when you had to go without extra money, a change of clothes and a sack of food, without weapons, dependent on others' hospitality—that time, when you were so ill provisioned, did you lack anything?"

Obviously they did. They doubtless grumbled when they couldn't find anyone to cook supper for them, groused when the nights grew cold, trembled when someone threatened them. But they answer with cheerful frankness, almost stupidly.

"No, nothing!"

And I believe that one day God will ask me the same thing.

"Lena, when I sent you out with the gospel, a single mother, with insufficient funds, when you had to struggle with pain and feeling abandoned, did you lack anything?" I have a strong sense that I will answer as they did. "No, nothing. Everything was great, just great."

A Woman and a Half

Rev 21:4; Isa 25:8; Mark 5:21–43; Lev 15; Num 19:11; Eph 5:9; Luke 10:30–37

I was talking about heaven with a group of children in my confirmation class from a school for the handicapped. We had a picture of people from all over the world who were dancing, and I said that all of us, God's friends, would be there too someday. Then nobody will need to cry, and nobody will be cruel. At that, there was a sudden joyful outburst among the whole group! It showed in their bodies, their arms, legs, and mouths!

"Then I'll push Anna's wheelchair," said one of them. Anna was severely afflicted with cerebral palsy and could not speak for herself.

"Wheelchairs are not allowed in heaven," I said.

Then such an uproar! Whoops and hollers, and chairs falling over. But Anna's friend stared hard at me with her small slanted eyes.

"You're trying to trick us, aren't you?" I had to agree of course. In heaven no one needs a wheelchair, because in heaven no one is sick, and everyone can jump and run and talk.

Uproar again, a joyful hullabaloo and hugging. Heaven opened up and all God's angels rejoiced to see us. Anna's friend looked at her own short, stubby hands and continued to think.

"Will I be able to type on a typewriter in heaven?" Absolutely! I assured her that she certainly would, if she needed to.

That glimpse of heaven, where each and every person is healed, such joy in a group used to being marginalized—that's how it must have been sometimes when Jesus healed the sick. But seeing it this way can be difficult for us who have heard those stories so often. More obvious to us apparently is the fact that Jesus breaks many taboos, and we are fine with that, so long as the taboos he breaks are not our own.

It is of course easy and even sometimes satisfying to moralize about sins that lie outside our sphere of competence or our ability to commit them. Shame and a pox on shell companies and on those who use them to embezzle millions. Or perhaps when our bodies are worn out, tired and old, we purse our lips like we were pulling knitting yarn through them, and we say, "Shame, for shame! These young people today, yelling all night long in the streets and breaking empty bottles in the park . . . !"

It's also easy to moralize about some other community's customs that seem cruel and primitive to us, as if doing so acquits us for our own culture's earlier ways for dealing with uncleanness and for ostracizing people. The biblical story of a grown woman and a nearly grown girl, both labeled unclean, shows this clearly. Jesus meets them on the same day. He is en route to the twelve-year-old girl, when the woman forces her way forward. She is bleeding, and she has been bleeding for a long time. And even though we do not know how much of the purity regulations in the Pentateuch apply in her case, we can sense her frightful experience of being excluded.

But we women of today have also been shamed; we have experienced the appalling humiliation of finding we have bled through our school uniform or our jeans. Nothing is as disgraceful as menstrual blood. In television commercials it is light blue, but in reality it is red and it stinks. We are still not able to pull out a tampon during a meeting and request a break, like someone else can pull out a cigarette and ask for a break. We do not have politically supported working conditions that take account of the way women's bodies are made to bear and give birth to new human beings. Painful menstruation and potential pregnancy are handicaps when a woman is looking for a job—so, how far have we really come?

Jesus, wonderful man, has no aversion to female blood. It costs him power to help the bleeding woman, but he does it anyway. Nor is he afraid of corpses. Although the twelve-year-old girl is already dead once he finally gets to her house, he is not put off by her lifeless body; he doesn't even seem to find the situation awkward. He simply walks up to her, takes her hand, and helps her back to life.

When it comes to dead bodies, we haven't come very far either. We doll them up with cosmetics and pay a complete stranger to wash them and lay them out. And on the other hand, we are fascinated with death and gory violence—seeking it as entertainment on television and in newspapers and books.

But perhaps we find ourselves horrified by the idea that this young twelve-year-old girl will soon be regarded as ready for marriage, and will be forced into it. Perhaps we are thinking of her being compelled to do the hard work of keeping house and home. If that's the case, then what are we doing today to ensure that such work is never forced on poverty-stricken women? I don't mean housework done with modern appliances. I'm talking about all the heavy work of producing what a family needs—which often means working a farm with primitive tools on a poor patch of land—and then preparing meals. Or perhaps it's the early commencement of sexual duty that we think is so shocking. But even now, many twelve-and thirteen-year-olds are forced into it by a teen-culture they certainly did not create on their own, a children's culture with Barbie and sexy girls' clothing beginning with sizes appropriate for seven-year-olds. And for that matter, there are tough-guy leather jackets for baby boys! Become like children, he once said to the adults. Perhaps he is saying today, "Let the children be children. Do not sexualize them before their time. That's your role, not theirs."

There will always be people who follow the rules. Some of them are good, kind folks, and when they see that the rules aren't working right, they are able to make exceptions and find an alternative. These people are not dangerous. The dangerous ones are the bureaucrats we know, or merely see on television, those who say they have fulfilled everything and therefore are not responsible if others have fallen through the cracks. They are not responsible if the rules themselves (and the effort to follow and observe the rules, rather than paying attention to people) have injured many, sometimes unavoidably.

The Pharisees wanted righteousness and thought it was enough to follow the law and the nearly watertight system of rules that had been built up around it. Among them there were certainly good-hearted persons who had no problem making exceptions for those who were too poor, too small, too old, or for whom a rule quite simply was not intended. But then, as now, there were also many who preferred a lazy form of righteousness—rules and nothing but rules, no matter what. With no others did Jesus become as livid as he did with these, and among no others did he make such bitter enemies.

Mercy is what God wants, far more than rules, and sometimes in direct opposition to rules. A man traveling from Jerusalem down to Jericho fell among thieves and taught us precisely this. So, when it comes to evaluations in the kingdom of heaven, I no longer entertain such great hope for the priest. I'm equally anxious for the Levite. But for the one who ended up in the ditch I am less and less concerned. Mercy will flow over him like oil and wine in his wounds.

Go, says Jesus, and do as that foreigner did, the one who was not afraid of getting his hands dirty. But why? Why should we keep on doing good? Wasn't heaven opened up to us for Jesus' sake? Aren't we his already, saved without good works? Aren't we now living in the light of heaven's open door, in the light from the future?

Well of course we are! But that's precisely *why* we should keep on. Paul says it in various ways, time after time. You are children of the light; therefore do the works of light. You belong to the Lord Jesus; therefore conduct yourselves accordingly. Of all the good that needs to be done in the world, consider what you can do, and then do it. And then let your good work go; think no more about it. Let it land wherever it is needed, on that other person, for instance, the one lying in the ditch.

Then immediately forget it; do not let your left hand know what your right hand is doing. There's no time for that. Forgetting about it also makes it easier for the man, woman, or child who falls into the hands of thieves to love the one who shows them mercy— for then we are *their* neighbor, and we cannot live without *their* love.

This Is My Body

It is September
and over the fields
the poppies
still open wounds.
It soothes.

For from within the darkness
I can see
that even what is broken
is beautiful.
And my heart is glad.

So I sit
in the sun
and let the wind
whisper to me
what I cannot comprehend.

The Beautiful
(Eccl 3:11)

Try to See Me!

Matt 14:1–42; Isa 40:3–8; Isa 42:1–4; John 1:29; Matt 11:2–6; Luke 13:6–9; John 4:14; 2 Kgs 4:42–44; Exod 3:14

It is a bright spring day. There is grass, new and fragrant. The Passover is near.[23] It is a terrible day. A day like those we know all too well. A day when the silent scream rises within us and fills our entire skull: Why is there no one to help *me*? He hears the news in the morning, when the Baptist's disciples come. We've already buried him, they say, with his head severed from his body. The horror of it ran in shivers up and down our backs.

John is no more—what now of all they had shared? Did they not sit together once long ago, their young heads bent over the Scriptures, searching out their calling? And Isaiah answered them— with the voice that cries out in the wilderness and prepares the way. With the voice of *him* who is not heard in the streets, the unknown one who does not break the bent reed, who does not snuff out the flickering flame. Did they not smile to each other and nod knowingly? Didn't John's dour, rugged mug break into a grin of recognition when he called out: "Behold, the Lamb of God!"

Someone, at least, saw him for who he was. Someone other than himself understood what he must be about and what he must become. Family and friends, people in general, found him utterly baffling. But there was at least one person who reassured him—although, in chained a dungeon, even that reassuring one doubted, needing to be reassured himself. My friend, you are so right, and at the same time so wrong. The eyes of the blind shall be opened and the ears of the deaf shall hear—but I do not come with punishment, or with the retribution of God. The ax rests for now against the root, and the fruitless tree will be allowed to stand one more year.

Yet now his friend is gone, that one who truly saw him, who saw him almost as he saw himself. It is a devastating loss, for I am thoroughly convinced that "seeing" is the most important thing one person can give to another, more important than tenderness, fellowship, or praise. And by all means more important than a disgusting love full of beautiful lies.

He is human like us, and now he needs some time to be alone, just as we would. But this deserted country is full of people, five thousand men—not counting the women and children, of course. The knot in his stomach loosens, not from weeping, but from compassion. Like a spring within him, gushing up to eternal life. He forgets himself for the moment—he comforts, helps, provides, and heals.

And now, of course, they are hungry. For an instant, it is as if he is fed up with the whole thing. As if the cry rises once more: Why doesn't anyone help *me*? Can't you guys do something for these people? Why don't *you* give them something to eat?—Oh, no! We can't do it.—Well, then, fine. I'll do it myself. Give them to me. Give me the five loaves and the two fish.

This story has to do with the Lord Jesus, but it also touches on two undeniably valid demands arising from the women's movement. The first of them is this: Look at *me*! See me as I am! See me as I see myself! Allow me, *me*, to define myself. I don't want to be defined by your desires or your need, by your condemnations, or your traditions! Look at *me*!

This, of course, is a deeply human desire. It is the same as that expressed by the child who doesn't want to be compared with a sibling. Or by the man who believes that we are caricaturing him and his brothers. It is a central issue in every struggle for human rights.

The second of these demands is the demand for respect toward our bodily needs. The stomach can be filled with weeping and compassion—or it can be empty. Our Lord never, ever, forgets our empty stomachs, not then and not now. He had one himself. God became a human being, God became a body, and God's church has not grasped the enormity of that truth.

Today is the day of bread—and it is the day of hunger. The bread which we break . . . as we say in the Eucharist. More and more I wonder whether we are really celebrating Holy Communion if we do not break *all* bread with the poor, if our strivings do not increasingly result in a total solidarity—with hungry bodies, with the invisible people.

The communion wafer is of no help to us in our failure to understand body and solidarity; the wafer is as non-sensual, non-bodily, and non-incarnational as any bread we could imagine. How I wish the church smelled of spring today, of new-mown grass, of grain, and an oven and spices. Perhaps it would help us to remember Jesus' insistence that no altar bread was too holy to eat, and that no bodily thing was too profane to hold God's interest.

It is also a day like any other day, when bodies are despised, abused, or murdered. No women's movement can rest until there is no more violence against women's bodies, until day and night, home and street, are safe. God took on a body and God himself is violated when children and women are raped or degraded through prostitution. God's creation is polluted when girls are discarded, or when they are aborted as fetuses or as newborns of the wrong gender.

Today, he who himself was a body sees our bodies, vulnerable and exposed to contempt—even the contempt we feel for our own; he sees them subject to sickness, stress, and aging. He sees the perversion of our culture, where our children and grandchildren grow up either hating their bodies or worshiping them, where they succumb

to anorexia and anabolic steroids, where they live with porno-
graphic violence and obsession with weight-loss and health.

He who himself was a body was helpless, both in the hands of
his mother and in the hands of his executioners. But he also experienced the joy of dancing and the strength of his arms when he
worked with the carpenter's tools or wrestled with his younger siblings. He had eyes that watched the pattern of swallows' flight
against the sky and ears that listened to their twittering. His nose
could be gladdened at the aroma of a campfire; his tongue enjoyed
the taste of grilled fish, and his skin felt the caress of wind, water,
and kind hands.

But he who was a body was never merely a body, and he never
sees us as mere bodies, no matter how much we see ourselves that
way, no matter how much our husbands, children, or culture may
look at us that way. He knows that we need to be seen at a deeper
level, just as he did.

For precisely this day, this horrible day, changes his story. It is
near Passover, the second Passover, and now he turns his feet toward
the final Passover. Now he ceases to instruct the crowds; this year he
concentrates his efforts instead on getting his nearest friends to understand. This day, this very night his life will change. He sends
them home, both the crowds whose stomachs he has satisfied and
the disciples in the boat. He goes up into the mountain to be alone
and to pray. I believe God helps him as God has helped us. I hope
he can cry. But I also know that God cannot take the place of a
flesh-and-blood friend.

When he comes down from the mountain, he is desperate for
another person who can see him, for another person's affirmation.
In darkness and against the wind, he goes to those from whom he
hopes the most. But as he approaches they fail to see that it is he.
They see a ghost! He calls to them. Don't be afraid; it's only me!
Don't be afraid; I am God!

Now for the first time, just when John has been taken from him, he applies to himself the name of God from the burning bush. Look at me! There is no danger here! Indeed, the dangerous thing is to fail to see me for who I am! I am God! Try to understand!

Do they? Not at all. Peter is as childish as ever: Let me come out there with you! I want to do that too! I want to take charge!— And so it continues, through the predictions of suffering, the Mount of Transfiguration, and Caesarea Philippi. Does anyone really see him? Hardly. Perhaps for a fleeting moment now and then, like glimpsing something out of the corner of the eye, like a terrifying premonition.

It is a horrible night; it is a splendid night. He reveals this night his deepest humanity, his need to be seen, as he discloses his innermost divine nature. Here the union of God and humanity is manifested in him. And nowhere do I love him as much as I do now, in the darkness, in adverse winds and waves and sorrow, when he cries out: Try to see me!

Unguarded

Prov 9:1–6; Matt 5:45; John 15:5; 1 Cor 10:16–17; 2 Cor 3:16–18;
Luke 22:14–20

It was an August evening at the church's camp outside the city.
Troops of scouts had been out on a hike and now returned in their
canoes, dragging them up onto the beach. They filed past a table
laden with sandwiches and milk and drifted on into the large as-
sembly room in the new lodge. They were typical teenagers, noisy
and boisterous, loose-jointed and uncoordinated, all arms and legs,
with young, pimply faces, sunburned, freckled, and peeling. We had
lit a fire and laid out a communion table with red wine in a glass
chalice and homemade bread. The aroma of rye and anis blended
with the smell of wet socks and burning wood. In short order, the
floor was completely covered with youngsters.

I could see that there would be no room for me to get around
to each individual, and after consulting with the leaders, I came to a
hurried decision. We would have to let them pass around the bread
and wine themselves, and to say the words to each other, even if it got
a little sloppy. But it turned out not to be sloppy at all; instead they
became completely quiet. The sun, hanging low, came in through
the window and lit up the red wine from Carmel, turning it to fire
and jewels.

Thus we laid the day in our open hands, its troubles, stupidity,
and loneliness, our joy at the sunshine, the water, and friendship, and
let it all fly up into God's hands, up through the open fireplace, to-

gether with the sparks from the dry wood. And when they had heard
the words and I had passed the salver and goblet to those closest to
me, they turned to one another with great seriousness. Some of them
used the prescribed liturgy, "Given for you, poured out for you." Some
of them spoke as they understood it, as it evolves when it is processed
in the soul: "This is Christ for you, like, his body, okay? You remember, right? His blood. Be careful with it!" Words of a covenant deeper
and greater than any scouting oath were carried from one to another,
linking them all to each other in a chain—even to the pastor, who
shrank a little into herself.

> *"Here. There's some left for you, too!" A grubby little girl with radiant
> eyes held out to me life and blessedness, the forgiveness of sins. And later,
> standing at the door, I received their intimate little shoves and greetings,
> as she and the others slipped out into the darkness to set up their tents.*

> *"You, uh—we, like, came close to each other, you know?"*

> *"It was a good thing we were so tired. We couldn't guard ourselves
> against God like we usually do!"*

It was powerful; I was completely shaken and had to sit for a
while on the porch steps and watch the stars coming out faintly high up
in the night sky. So much of the Eucharist's mysteries had become clear.

The setting sun, so banal in the telling and in pictures, made it
sovereignly obvious how the divine had fallen upon the earthly and
spread rest and tenderness around itself, right into our hearts. And
giving something for our bodies as well, like sandwiches and lumpy
sleeping bags. Eucharist is like a magnifying glass, through which
the burning sun of God's love is concentrated, the love that causes
the sun itself to shine and rain to fall on the just and the unjust,
and showers itself upon us right here where God meets us in grain
from the fields and in grapes from the mountains.

We had just been so near to one another, belonging together so
closely, even though the next morning they wouldn't know what to

say to me, and I wouldn't be able to tolerate their music or their noisiness. It is simply the way of the Eucharist: it is a togetherness that has nothing to do with whether we like each other or even know one another, or whether we share our lives or interests; it is a togetherness through him who is the vine, the only living tree, of which all of us, together and individually, are branches.

This life together in the same tree, generation after generation throughout the earth, seems like what had happened on this evening, though most of the time it isn't. Yet it is always there, a single life, a single loaf, a single body. It doesn't matter if we don't recognize it or always see it. But anyone who refuses to share Holy Communion with another Christian does violence to the bread, the bread that is his body already broken.

"Like, unguarded," she had said. Exactly. Here if anywhere we can lay aside all masks, all attempts to be greater or better than we are. Not only do we have fellowship, but we also find a very special sort of solitude in the Eucharist, for I am addressed in it as an individual and I meet the Lord without the protection of the group. It can be frightening to be exposed before the Holy, but there is also an incredible rest to be had in letting go all the roles we play and all our absurd posturing.

I believe that this meeting is like our meeting with him in death—provided we dare to let go our grip, to drop the masquerade. For whatever death may be, it is at least this: I meet him without the slightest possibility of hiding myself or covering up. Yet I am secure, recognizing what it is I face in death: for he who meets us in death is the one we met in the bread when we were defenseless, the one who gave himself for us there, the one who gave himself up to death in order to win life for us all.

A thrush began to sing above the roof just now. I remember earlier spring times, when the song of the thrush cut me like a knife, and I remember why. But I no longer feel the knife. It had to do with a memory, of course, but today it survives only as the memory of a memory. It would scarcely have had even a bluish tone of melancholy, if this spring evening itself had not reminded me of it and brought to mind how long ago some things were and how painful it could be for a young person.

"You remember, right?" the boy had said to the one next to him. "In remembrance of me," said Jesus. In remembrance of what happened, that's why we do this. No, it's more like a commemoration, a matter of drawing what once happened into what is happening now, so that we hear him speak it quite near to us, as recently as last night.

When that night came for Jesus, the night in which he was betrayed, he took bread and wine and said, "Remember me. Remember that I was in the darkness." It was God who was here; it was God who felt the pain in his body from the nails and torture. It was God who wept in anticipation of the unavoidable. It was God who was left alone, without any human help.

Remember that I walked here on the earth. Since then, everything is different. Remember that I washed your feet—since then, no work is despised. Remember that I spoke with the children and the women—since then, no one is superior to anyone else, neither here in the world or in the presence of God. Remember that I forgave the thief and invited myself to the home of Zacchaeus. Since then, there are no hopeless cases. Not then and not now. There is always forgiveness available; we are never without a way to God. It is never any farther back to God than it is to the next Eucharist.

This Bread, This Wine

Eph 2:10; 1 Chr 29:14; Isa 1:11–15; Amos 5:21–24; John 15:1–10; Col 1:24

There is something at this time of year that is very typical of God: it is the phenomenon of constant return. New spring seasons come to us with starlings, larks, and coltsfoot. God doesn't weary of illness or darkness, as we do, nor does he give in to cruelty, his own or anyone else's. God returns. He returns to us, in fact, over and over again, ready to forgive or to assign us something new to do. The wood anemones that cover our hills in abundance and the woodpecker that drums for life and love with a holy staccato, as he does every spring, are like forgiveness. And this eternal creating of life and forgiveness, this is something only God can do. Our creating, our forgiveness are pale images of his.

Yet in all earthly existence there is a good collaboration between God and human beings. When we bear children and raise them up, when we sow clover and set potatoes, build schools and pass legislation, we do it together with God, who sees to it that we are able. "For we are what he has made us, created in Christ Jesus for good works, which God prepared beforehand to be our way of life."

We say it a little childishly, but perhaps also with astonishment and joy, when we offer up the collection at a worship service: "We give thee but thine own." In fact, everything we have, we have only received, and we give back little enough—though when we do give back, we do so through giving to other people. It is a very strange arrangement, this covenant between God and humanity. We transgress it most readily when we do injustice to our neighbor. There are always three parts making up the alliance between God and me. If righteousness and mercy do not dwell among us, then all our prayers and worship can never help us, no matter how elegant we make them. They only nauseate God, say the prophets.

This doesn't mean that we should quit praying. Evil is a spiritual power; it strikes out against the people of the earth, damaging their bodies, shriveling their souls, and confusing them in mind and spirit. Paying no attention whatsoever to the proportion of ill deeds an individual has done, harm most often strikes small bodies, little children who are malformed or stricken with cancer as a result of Chernobyl[24] or crippled from landmines or bombs all over in the world.

Everything we humans are capable of, whatever we can do to heal bodies and souls, is needed in our collaboration with God. The spiritual power we have to contribute is our prayers, our stubborn, persistent, obstinate prayers. Spring, too, illustrates the defiance of prayer and faith: the blue anemone that glows among the faded leaves, the lapwing that moves in daring sweeps over the frozen fields with snow still in the furrows, long before the soil is habitable. This is how we are to pray in spite of everything, to cry out even when we think that we can no longer live or endure, just like the lapwing cries out to us about the hard luck of life.

We can speak of collaboration in the bread and wine as well, by which we gave our work in sowing and harvest, in baking and winemaking—but where we also could not have done a thing without God. The demarcation between what I do and what God does is a little artificial, all the more so when we begin to talk about power. We often hear in devout circles that when we come to the end of our own strength, we can draw upon God's. Such nonsense! As if *all* power is not God's power, the power that keeps my heart pumping blood and my lungs breathing air, the power that moves my heart to pray and my lungs and my spirit to cry out to God.

I see before me the vine, the vine that he is, and our connection with him. It makes it easy to see that there is only one power, like the sap in the tree, only one life, the life of the branches in the tree, their connection to root and trunk. On a difficult evening the question comes to me: "Is there also only one pain? Do we share the same pain, he and I?" If so, then it's pure madness when I isolate it and keep it to myself, when I call it mine, mine, *mine!* It's no less insane than to speak of "my life," or "my strength." Perhaps my pain is a part of his, and perhaps conversely he reckons my pain as his own. Perhaps I can bear a portion of the pain he continually carries in agony over our poor world. I don't know, but I think it could be so.

Quite a few years ago, I read something by Birgitta Trotzig[25] regarding what we offer in Holy Communion: this bread—our work, and this wine—our pain. Her words caused me to start thinking along another line. For, of course, it's true that I offer my work to God. In the evening after a good day, my prayer runs something like this: "We were able to accomplish so much together today, God, you and I. It's so nice when I am able to work. Thank you for that, and forgive me for what didn't turn out so well. And now receive my day and accept my work."

But a day of pain is more dismal, more difficult and more grueling than a day of work. I don't care to have such days; I'd rather follow the geese, as they fly away northward to the wastelands, crying, "Come with us! Come with us!" Yet shouldn't I also be able to offer a day like this to God? Yes! I should be able to hand it to him and say, "Here, take my day. Here, receive my pain. I'm not thankful for it, but here it is."

What might he do with it . . . ?

Bread for Tomorrow

Matt 6:9–13; Exod 16:16; Matt 6:34; Ps 23; Mark 1:15; Luke 17:21; Eph 1:22–23; Eph 1:14; 2 Cor 1:22; 2 Cor 5:5, Mark 13:14–20

When the new Swedish translation of the New Testament was published in 1981, there were some features of it that proved especially troubling to readers. But one of the most troubling of them compelled us to think about the prayer for bread, and that was good in itself. "Give us today our bread for the coming day":[26] what is that supposed to mean? Does it have to do with planning ahead, with the fact that Jesus sometimes simply seems opposed to making plans? Or perhaps it's about anxiety for tomorrow, which for many of us is the same thing.

Some scholars think that the Lord's Prayer is to be read as an eschatological text, that it deals with the last times. If so, it would imply that Jesus taught it to his disciples in the conviction that his time was short, that all time is short, both the world's and ours, and that he would return very soon to finish what he began.

I think it's worth testing such a reading. It is certainly obvious that he felt himself short of time. Besides, the Lord's Prayer often becomes mere rote doggerel for us, since we recite it so often and scarcely ever hear anymore what we say in it. It would be good to think a bit about these familiar words.

The expression *Our Father* has become in our minds almost the equivalent of saying "God is everyone's dad." But "our" here means Jesus' father, and because of Jesus, my father too; it doesn't mean the father of every human being, without qualification. Thus: God, you are the one the Lord Jesus calls father. It is he who is nearest to your heart; it is he who has made you known, and because of him, we also may say, "Our Father."

In heaven. "Heaven" can refer to the area where God has power, both on earth and among humanity. But primarily the word means that God is not earthly, created, like us. God belongs to another sphere, another dimension. A better expression for helping us correctly understand this introductory phrase would be "heavenly father."

There now follow three petitions, which are actually three sides of the same thing, and which resemble the Jewish Prayer of Mourning, the kaddish. In the contemporary version of the Prayer Book, that prayer begins like this: "Glorified and sanctified be God's great name throughout the world which He has created according to His will. May He establish His kingdom in your lifetime and during your days, and within the life of the entire House of Israel, speedily and soon." Jesus expresses the same thing, only in a slightly different form.

Hallowed be your name. What does it mean to hallow a name? It can't be such a simple matter as avoiding swear words. We get a better idea of the meaning if we compare alternative renderings of Psalm 23. The NRSV in traditional fashion translates it, "He leads me in right paths for his name's sake." The New Living Translation, on the other hand, puts it like this: "He guides me along right paths, bringing honor to his name." One's name and one's honor go together. We are praying, then, that people will realize that God is active and deserves due credit for all the benefits of the creation sustained. We should not give the honor to anyone (or anything) else for what God has done.

Your kingdom come. The kingdom of God appeared like the dawn when Jesus began to announce, "The kingdom of God is near; it is in your midst; it is within you; it has begun—but *only* begun." Here we pray for the fullness of the kingdom, for its appearance in the full light of day. This is what theologians refer to as "the already and the not yet," and it can seem a little tricky. But an elderly pastor explained it well for me when he said, "You will never understand this unless you have a long engagement. It took seven years before I got my own parish and we were able to get married."

Your will be done. Perhaps a child can explain it: If everybody in the world were like Jesus we wouldn't have any problems, right? Exactly! So these three petitions are an expression of the same thing. We pray that God's honor, kingdom, and will would be in sole control, that the day would come when everything is placed under God's control, on earth as in heaven.

When God's kingdom does come, it will be important that we are ready, and so we pray: *Give us today our bread for the coming day.* This petition has been the most difficult for translators to deal with, for no one knows exactly what the word translated "the coming day" means. There is much to say for rendering it, "tomorrow's bread." In this way the words take on the flavor of not being concerned for more than one day at a time, as well as the flavor of the Eucharist. It's thus a multifaceted prayer: Let us not profane any food and always remember him who was broken on the cross. Let all bread we eat, no matter what sort, be heavenly bread! Give us confidence in the face of every coming day.

But we remember too the lines of a hymn: "We taste the future the poor look for, the day when the walls come down." We taste the bread that comes down from heaven; we're given a foretaste of heaven. The Spirit is sometimes likened in the New Testament to an advance payment (although now the Greek word *arrabon* is more often translated "guarantee"). "It is God who establishes us with you in Christ and has anointed us, by putting his seal on us and giving us his Spirit in our hearts as a first installment." I believe that this "first installment" is what we sometimes feel—when our heart comes to a sense of peace at a graveside, when we are gripped with enthusiasm for some good thing, or when new tenderness wells up within us. This is a foretaste of heaven.

But above all, that "coming day" is *the* Coming Day, the last day, the ultimate day, the greatest day of all. So we should probably pray for the heavenly bread like this: "Give us today the bread of the Great Tomorrow."

And forgive us our debts, as we also have forgiven our debtors. This petition becomes easy enough to understand when we hear it in this "eschatological" perspective. It has to do with the ancient insight: I could die tonight, so I should leave things in proper shape when I go. Let my accounts be in good order when the day comes to close the books.

And do not bring us to the time of trial. Here it is again, the testing that is so difficult that we despair of passing it. Or the Testing he spoke of, the day when we will have to flee into the mountains, when everything holy will be profaned, the frightful time that must come before the dawn of Tomorrow. May we escape it!

But rescue us from the evil one is just another way of saying the same thing. Rescue us from what can take away our faith and confidence, save us from everything the evil one can think of doing.

So then, we can pray something like this:

Heavenly father, you who are our father for Jesus' sake, just as you are his,

we pray that things on earth will be like they are in heaven,

that you will receive all honor, that your kingdom will come in fullness, that your will be done in all things.

Give us now, today, Tomorrow's bread,

and when that day comes, let us both receive forgiveness and have offered forgiveness.

Bring us not into the Great Day of Testing, but save us from that Evil.

We can close with the words of the Jewish kaddish:

"*Blessed and praised, glorified and exalted, extolled and honored, adored and lauded be the name of the Holy One, blessed be He, beyond all the blessings and hymns, praises and consolations that are ever spoken in the world.*"

Mary's Annunciation

Luke 1:26–38; Mark 6:3; Luke 2:22–24, cf. Lev 12

I catch a glimpse of Mary through the bare branches of the birch trees. It was just about this time that she became pregnant, just as the buds were beginning to swell. But it isn't easy to get a good look at her behind all the words and pictures. She stands there hidden behind our songs, legends, traditions, and prejudices.

Sometimes the tradition shows us a virgin mother, one who her whole life long is young, passive, innocent, almost unearthly. *Semper virgo* perhaps—forever a virgin—though that's not a particularly Protestant perspective. No, we may not want an eternal innocence in her, but we do want something along those lines just the same. Something to answer our infantile need for a mother we can call our very own, one who isn't pulled in several directions, who doesn't have many children, and who has no interests of her own.

We have seen innumerable depictions of Mary and her firstborn, as well as of a Mary engaged in acceptable housekeeping duties. There is, for example, the wonderful fourteenth-century painting from Buxtehude, portraying Mary with her knitting, which she's holding a little incorrectly. But we have no picture of her mucking out the donkey's stall, or slaughtering a hen. There is no scene of Mary reasoning with Joseph about how to make the housekeeping budget stretch to the end of the month, or of her embracing him. Nothing of a Mary breastfeeding one baby after another after another (she apparently had at least seven).

We have placed other labels on her as well, not the least of them being "humble," although the Bible never calls her that. If we imagine that "humble" implies submissiveness, or having no opinion of one's own, or saying "poor little old useless me," then it doesn't work. But if we use it to mean knowing how small—and how big—one is in the presence of God, then it works fine. But "humble" is a misused word, one we need to be careful with. "Obedient," on the other hand, is a better word if we mean by it that a person tries to become what God wants, what God has planned. Mary risks losing all her personal security and obeys God. In this she is like her son.

"Weakness," "lowliness"—these are words the newer hymns are full of. We have to wonder whether these hymn writers have ever met grown girls on the verge of womanhood and seen how strong they are. Are we ever stronger, in body and independence? Do we have such a low opinion both of girls generally and of the relative poverty Mary lived in? Is the body of a young woman the most un-Godlike thing these hymn writers can imagine? Do they use this symbol to make Mary's pregnancy as strange as possible?

The more current pictures are of the strong, courageous, and independent Mary. But we really don't know whether she was like this either. Of course, the image echoes the need we strong women have to identify ourselves with someone who stands near to God. So we slap another label on Mary according to our need, and it is just as much an outrage as every other time we use another person, living or dead, for our own aims.

At the end of the day, we get only a inkling of her. An ordinary Jewish girl, about fifteen years of age. Fully capable of keeping house, properly engaged to a nice guy, one who wants to obey God. A guy who takes her into his home, even though there will be no "wedding night" until Candlemas,[27] when the days of her purification are complete. And he does what so many of us have done, he also takes into his home a child who from the start is not his own. And we observe how love, affectionate care, and living together create the nearness that truly makes a child our own, regardless of biological connections.

For now comes the miracle. God becomes a human being. God becomes a body, in the same way as we all do, from an embryo to a fetus to a child. God *wants* to become a human, and that is truly a miracle. But what about the virginity, then? Indeed, we've made it unnecessarily difficult, for if God were to ask us anything today or at the gates of heaven, it would hardly be whether we could understand the virgin birth. More likely God wonders what we do with the children whose lives and fate actually are in our hands: children, grandchildren, students, children on television, needy children in bordellos and refugee camps.

This is a much more important question than whether Jesus could begin growing in Mary's womb without a male sperm cell. I believe that he could; I believe that God can do whatever God wants to do. I also think that it is simply stupid to say that God is able, whenever something happens a little out of the ordinary. God who bears the world and creates the Milky Way and small children, who brings forth new spring seasons in the earth and new affection in us—God can do this. But that doesn't mean I know that God has actually done it this particular time.

But all of us ought to consider what the Virgin Birth implies. It can't mean hostility toward sex, for a virgin birth was completely unthinkable in the Judaism of the day. It can imply that Jesus belongs to yet another outsider group, that he is one of the illegitimates, which is less important today than the fact that he was also a refugee child. Or perhaps it is meant to demonstrate that from the very beginning he chose a woman to bear what is most important, from this pregnancy and even to the proclamation of the empty tomb.

In any case, it reminds us that God created body and soul in an indissoluble unity and was delighted with it. Christianity does not regard the body as a despised dwelling for the soul. God made the body, my own and yours, utterly original and not at all evil; the real problem lies somewhere else. Look at your hands, and you'll see what I mean. We use them to caress and to strike, to carry the children and the grocery bags, to stir a pot and to knead bread, to work with a dish cloth, a hymnal and a pen, to hang on to money and to give it away.

When God became a human being, God became a physical body. This is why all bodies are worthy of our respect, though not of our idolization; there is scarcely anything more important to emphasize today. Anorexia. Anabolic steroids. Dieting. Face lifts. Violence. Wife-killings. Sexual exploitation. Rape. All this speaks another language, one of denial, self-hatred, fear of growing old, lust for power and control, and a lack of gratitude for the body God gave.

Now I see her better, this Mary. What is she saying to me? Something like this: "I stand here with a new life in my womb. I have stopped having my period; I'm pregnant. And there you stand, no longer having periods either, because your womb is too old for it now. Life has at last embroidered your experiences in your face, working it in as cross-stitching at the corners of your eyes and mouth. And all of this, the blood and uterus, wrinkles and aging, have been so difficult both for your religion and mine. But isn't it wonderfully fun that God has given us bodies? Don't let anyone despise you because of your body or your experiences!

"My son will soon be born and his hands will be so small as they grip mine, his body so light and warm against my shoulder. Through his skin, his nose, through his eyes and ears and mouth, he will take in his world. Soon, all too soon, my son will die and I will no longer be able to take his hands. Someone else will grab them brutally, hold them down and drive nails through them. This is how God chose to become a human being, and this is why we are never alone in the suffering of body or soul. This is why we do not give up."

Barbed Wire in Snow

Rom 8:19–21; Acts 17:28; Ps 148

I was about ten or eleven years old and tramping through the snow with my Uncle Sven, who was a forest ranger. He had something he wanted to show me and had come home on purpose to get me. The weather was raw and the snow was heavy; I did my best to put my little boots in his big footprints. We emerged from the woods into a field with a stone wall on the other side. There she lay, a dead doe. Prostrate, with a slender, elegant hoof in the air, tangled in barbed wire, and her neck stretched backwards in a silent shriek. Even in the midst of death, she seemed to move with grace and desperation.

"This oughta be outlawed," said Sven, "people leaving old wire on their property like this, and where we don't use it to fence in cows anymore. But it's hard to get it cleaned up. Nobody's really interested in doing anything about it. Poor thing—she suffocated."

Where the path continued on, the barbed wire was rolled up a bit, and lay half hidden in the snow. Here and there the fence posts had been broken off or fallen over from some other cause. It was hard for me to trace the line of wire in the snow.

I remember that a fox had been there and ripped out a bit of her belly. But mostly I remember the sockets where her eyes had been pecked out by a raven or a crow—and while she was still alive, because they were bloody—though fortunately I didn't understand that at the time.

Sven was watching me like a person does when he gives someone a present and is waiting for her to open it and either to accept it
or not. Apparently he was satisfied with what he saw, for we went
back to the car to let the dog out, and we took a swing down to the
lake to fish for pike through the ice.

In many ways that was another time in the history of the earth,
a time before David Attenborough[28] and waste recycling, before the
Silent Spring[29] and Chernobyl, before humanity had really begun the
fastest mass eradication of other living creatures the world has ever
seen. We could swim anywhere and drink from any stream, and take
the bus everywhere. Thor Heyerdahl[30] sailed the Kon-Tiki on the
currents of a clean ocean, and no one dreamed of the possibility
that the Gulf Stream could ever alter its path because of the way
human activity would lead to global warming. Socrates long ago
had complained of deforestation in Greece—but he had no inkling
of what it would do to the ground water. For that matter, we have
scarcely begun to realize it ourselves.

It was also another time in my own life, although I have always
loved the earth and most of all the trees and large birds. I love the
universe with stars and black holes and bent space. I have never
feared any created thing—other than human beings.

I am unable to regard our environment as our "milieu,"
objectified and distinct from us, something that exists for our sake
and something we can destroy or preserve in the way we do our
possessions. It's rather nature that preserves us, that is the foundation and prerequisite for our bodily existence—and a bodily existence is the only existence we have. The rest of the living creatures
of the earth can get along just fine without us, but we could never
survive without them.

I saw Lucy, our Ethiopian primordial mother, in the National
Museum in Addis Ababa, and I felt dizzy. I sometimes think about
the joy God must have felt, after waiting millions and billions of

years, when the first glimmer of consciousness kindled itself in a human eye. And I can sense even in myself—and perhaps in God—the anxiety of every other created being in the face of this double-minded being who would have the power to choose and who would so often choose ill and thus draw down death and condemnation upon all creation.

There is a power in the grass and healing in sitting under a tree or on the shore of the sea. It has nothing to do with God's being somehow *in* the grass or the sea or the sighing of a tree, in some kind of animistic or pantheistic fashion. It has to do instead with the fact that the fir trees and the cows, the water and the spiders, and all other things are in God, just as we are. "In him we live and move and have our being." But we human beings are in revolt; we are the disobedient element of creation. Everything else is purer than we are, and there are times when we can actually taste that purity.

For this reason it is good to pour leftover wine on the earth and to give unused Eucharist bread to the sparrows, who know that when they fall, they fall in God's hand. There is so much in life that involves daring to fall, even into the darkness, so much that involves the confidence that no matter how hard or in what direction we fall, God is there. Sparrows know it. Likewise the wheat we make bread from ripens unresistingly and knows when the time for harvest has come, knows that God is a harvester to be relied upon.

"Praise the Lord, sun and moon; praise him, all you shining stars!" But of course, we hardly need to remind them to do this! Our songs of praise are fragmentary and intermittent. Whenever we get around to raising them, they form a part of the universal praise coming perpetually from all creation. This is why we commit the unspeakable when we destroy our earth, our mother.

It was another time of year when Uncle Sven and I walked through the snow. Today, as the days and nights grow equal in length, a six-year-old and I go out for a walk in search of the finch that for now is still stumbling around in the universal opera of praise. For the most part, it's sparrows that are chattering under the bare hedges, but the blueberry branches are budding under the dirty snow and they open up when we bring them inside.

It's not far from Lund out to the surrounding farmlands; the sky is blue today above the open earth. The black-headed gulls haven't arrived yet to follow in clouds behind the tractors, but the crows, jackdaws, and rooks are there, with their black and grey wings.

"There are too many of them," says the child. "How come?"

It's not such a strange question; the child has grasped the cyclical nature of things.

"There aren't enough hawks and eagles," I answer.

"Some idiots probably shot them," she says.

Exactly. It's nice that someone gets it.

A Magnificent Little Man

Luke 12:49–50; Luke 11:29; Matt 9:9–10; Luke 11:37–42; Luke 14:1–14; Luke 19:1–10; Luke 11:14–16; Matt 22:1–14; Isa 25:6–8

Another party! I almost wouldn't have believed it possible. He's been so short of time, so tense, sometimes openly disappointed that there hasn't been more of life. "I came to bring fire to the earth," he says, "and how I wish it were already kindled! I have a baptism with which to be baptized, and what stress I am under until it is completed!" And when he draws a big crowd, he is dismissive. You only want a sign, and you'll get no other sign than the sign of Jonah!

It doesn't sound like he was in the mood for a feast, although he has often enjoyed eating with both friends and strangers. Like the time Matthew got up from his tollbooth and invited home a crowd of people like himself, the sort that usually would not be included. Their joy was contagious surely, like Jesus' own was whenever he succeeded in getting someone back on an even keel. What fun they must have had that day!

Perhaps Jesus also enjoyed being with people at the bottom of the ladder, just for his own sake. For a person who endures great suffering, one who is either currently in or soon headed for suffering, a person who lives with integrity, it is pleasant and relaxing to be with other disillusioned, cast-off folks. We know this well enough from our own experience.

The pious sort got annoyed of course, and perhaps even for some in his own circle it took a while to get used to the idea that in order to be with Jesus you had to be prepared to be in bad company (assuming it was now even possible to be certain at all about what constituted bad company). For he found hypocrites the most tedious of all, those who regarded themselves as better, who thought that they were good enough as is. How embarrassing he must have been to his friends sometimes.

A Pharisee invited him home, and Jesus didn't have the good sense to wash himself with the water of purification, as was prescribed. The host was shocked, and so earned a stinging rebuke: You wash a cup and saucer, but what do you yourselves look like on the inside? You tithe herbs of all kinds, and neglect justice and the love of God!

Another Pharisee asked him to dinner one Sabbath, and an uninvited fellow showed up, his swollen body awkward and painful. Jesus tried to get the Pharisee and his friends to approve doing the right thing—in this case, of healing the man immediately—but they said nothing. So he restored the man to health in spite of them. And if that weren't enough, when later he saw how the guests were trying to grab the best seats, he started in on them. Not only embarrassing, but dangerous.

They now come to Jericho, already an ancient city even at that time. The day is quite warm, for the town lies in a depression some 800 feet below sea level, not far from the Dead Sea. It's already April, and both in and around the city flowers are in bloom in a way folks from Judea have scarcely ever seen. Jericho is an oasis in a desert land, with palms and sycamores lining the streets.

There is just one hill left to climb en route to Jerusalem, but it is long, steep, and difficult. To Bethany, the prominence outside Jerusalem for which they had presumably first set out, there is a gain in altitude of almost 3,600 feet, and a distance of more than twelve miles just by the way the crow flies, and the road is full of switchbacks. It can't be done in one day. They will have to find some place to spend the night.

As they enter the streets of Jericho, their luck is with them; someone wants to invite them home. Jesus spots him, a man who isn't too worried about his dignity, even though he is a businessman who owns the franchise for collecting the city's taxes; he is a rich and influential person. But his prestige, so important to a person in this culture, has to yield to his curiosity. He wants to see Jesus, and for that reason, he has climbed up into a sycamore. And Jesus calls to him. "Hustle up!"

Indeed, Zacchaeus, you do get moving, because Jesus wants to stay at your house. Whether this is why we are all so fascinated with you or not, I do not know, but you seem like an old friend. For you were little, and yet you were allowed to be along; you were so great that you were able to change. You let yourself be persuaded, and you ignored social conventions when he needed you and you needed him.

I'll bet it was some party you put on, for you had the means to do it. Food and drink and happy times—and relief among the disciples when they saw that Jesus was in a good mood again and they could think about something besides what was going to happen in Jerusalem. And of course all the unsuitable sort of people also got a share of the food and drink. No one was compelled just to stand outside and peek in enviously, unless they insisted on it.

Some people grumbled, naturally, but they had been grumbling a long time, but now you knew what you really wanted. You wanted to belong, for you are a child of Abraham, a child of righteousness, and righteousness had finally come to you at this party. Overwhelmed, you opened your heart and your purse, and the Lord rejoiced.

But watch out, Zacchaeus! When you open the door to righteousness, righteousness is what you get! It comes in many forms, according to each and every person's situation. In yours, it looks like this: give back what you took unfairly. Give half of all your goods to the poor. You have now been swept into the course of events, into the kingdom of God now underway. Be careful now, if you leave the door open. People will eat you out of house and home and skin you alive.

Not even the poor are always good—but you already know that full well, just from your professional experience. And perhaps your freedom looks like this: that with eyes wide open you allow yourself to be swindled out of an occasional ten-dollar bill.

This was his last party with people from outside. There would be a meal with his friends one evening in Bethany, but that would be different. And then the final evening in the Upper Room, the one he arranged on his own initiative. What he says at that event echoes back to all those other times when people had gathered to eat with him.

"I have eagerly desired to eat this Passover with you before I suffer!"

It is his eager desire to share this last evening with his closest friends. It is God's desire that righteousness will be celebrated in every home. It is a celebration that points forward, as they all do.

"I will not eat it again until it is fulfilled in the kingdom of God."

In the kingdom of God that began around Jesus, he invited himself time and time again into the homes of people like Zacchaeus. The fully manifested kingdom of God comes in time as a feast, as mighty a feast as a king puts on for his son's wedding. All of us unsuitable people are promised that we will eat together with him. The prophet Isaiah knew this long ago, of course.

On this mountain the LORD of hosts will make for all peoples a feast of rich food, a feast of well-aged wines. And he will destroy on this mountain the shroud that is cast over all peoples, the sheet that is spread over all nations; he will swallow up death forever. Then the Lord GOD will wipe away the tears from all faces, and the disgrace of his people he will take away from all the earth, for the LORD has spoken.

Seed and Harvest

In the midst of the verdure of late summer
the last harvest comes
into my thoughts.

And I weep,
not from sadness only,
but with a certain sweetness, too.

It is why I will not fear
when my broken straws are gathered
into the Harvester's final basket.

The Harvest
(Ps 126:5)

Always Open

Ps 103:8–14; Luke 15:1–32; Gen 22:1–14; Jas 1:12–13; Luke 10:22

Now that I've had children of my own, I have a better understanding of God and of the love of God. It is probably like the anxiety-filled love birthed within me at the birth of a child—whether born from my body, or in a far distant place—and they bring her to me and lay her on my arm or my stomach, and for the first time I meet that inscrutable gleam in her dark eyes. God's joy in us is probably like our joy, the joy that grows with an explosive power that can force its way through asphalt at least—and seems compelled to do it, at the *very* least.

Now I know what it is to love so much that I would do almost anything for my child. No one is allowed to harm her; she shall have it better than I did, and hang the cost. Now I know that God seeks us out just the way we look for a child who has gone lost; we stumble around in the woods, fir limbs slap us in the face, and our throats grow hoarse with calling and our eyes swell up with crying. Now I know the joy God feels over a child who is found safe and sound.

In fact, even God now knows more about what it's like to be an earthly mommy or daddy. God in heaven is incapable of being tired or flat broke, needs no sleep and is never without resources. But surely Jesus was dead tired from work sometimes, even when he was still at home in Nazareth. He was so poor during his years of wandering that he had to borrow everything, from a manger to a donkey, so poor that he had to accept board, room, and money from both friends and strangers. Thus now, in the heart of the Divine, there is a memory, and perhaps not merely a memory, of what it is to live and suffer pain in a body. But didn't God already know what that was like, since after all God always knows everything? I believe that in some respects, God knew this in the same way as a man knows that childbirth is painful, even though he hasn't personally experienced it.

Now both God and I know how infuriating it can be when things don't go right. God knows how I can say, "If you don't stop doing that right now, I'm never going to take you with me to town again!" And though the child doesn't stop, she gets to come along again, of course—for naturally I repent. We do find biblical references about God such as, "he will not keep his anger forever." Can God also repent? Isn't God unchanging?

Well certainly, God's personality is unchanging, but as usual we get into trouble when we try to analyze God with logic rather than in accordance with the fact that God is one who loves to the uttermost. God may be immutable, but God is not immovable—neither static nor unresponsive—when it comes to loving us.

Raising children makes all this much clearer. The toughest thing about raising children is to keep a proper distance: to avoid injuring their integrity, crippling their ability to act and to decide and to carry through. It's hard to see them do stupid things or get into difficulties, and yet to be unable to do much toward helping them. So hard not to abandon them, yet at the same time not to interfere either. Such a balancing game!

Is this also true of God? Yes, it is, if Jesus means us to understand that the father in the parable of the two sons is God. So many emotional sensations the father must have gone through as all this was unfolding—for in the parable he is one of us. When the young knucklehead asked for his portion of the inheritance, and while he then recklessly squandered it away, the father was thinking: "Has he fallen in with drug abusers? What if he gets AIDS? Is he on drugs

himself? Is he even still alive? Will he come home with values I cannot accept? Does he think that certain rules only apply to him—
which is the basic characteristic of the criminal mind?

And oh the joy when he does come home, the purest happiness
of all! Seeing, and not merely hoping, that the love, worry, and expense were not in vain is strengthened in the faith that love never
goes lost. The father is the same, even though anger, worry, anxiety,
and joy come and go; for that is what love looks like.

But now, what are we to do with that incurably sensible, uptight
rule-keeper? Hey, you older brother, you stay-at-home, you old
sourpuss—come on into the banquet hall and eat with us and
dance! You really should have given your little brother a hug even
before he had a bath. But it's never too late, you know. He forgives
you for everything. And then your dad takes you out on the front
porch: "Look!" he says. "There is plenty of everything here! The
earth is full of my glory, and all that is mine is yours."

Does God also repent in the dreadful story of Abraham offering up Isaac as a sacrifice? I really do not know. I cannot understand
Abraham as a father; I would have refused. Does God test faith by
treating Abraham like this? I don't believe it; God tempts no one.
And anyway, whose faith really needs to be tested further than it already is tested? Isn't life hard enough as it is? Isn't faith always a
matter of hanging on in spite of everything?

If someone tells me that I must kill my child, it isn't God
speaking; it's Satan. Or if it is some sort of god, it is not a god I can
accept. I would say, "I want nothing to do with you; you know
nothing of the love that was manifested in Jesus Christ."

Parenthood can also throw light on one of the liturgy's most
enigmatic formulations: "We give thanks, O Lord, that the way to
you is always open through Jesus Christ." It is what we say following
confession and absolution. We have laid all our burdens, our guilt
and humiliations alike, at the feet of God the Father. God removes

them and bears them for the sake of the Son, who counts us as his very best friends, his own brothers and sisters. But how can this be?

Imagine a youngster of six or so, standing at your front door with a bloody nose and tears streaming down his cheeks. He is your child's best pal, so you take him in, even though you know that he began the fight this time too, even though you don't have the time, and even though he gets blood on your newly ironed blouse when you comfort him. You do it not because you love him, but because he is your child's friend.

Or one morning ten years later you find him in a sleeping bag under the kitchen table, hung over. He has run away. He's made off with fifty dollars from some cashbox, and he wants to end it all, for he is young and cannot see any way out, cannot see that he is worth far more than fifty dollars. You put your arms around him, even though now it's *you* who barely come up to *his* shoulders, and you pay back the money he's taken. You may not do this because you want to save a life, but you do it because the boy is still your child's closest friend. You may not have any real desire to do this, but how could you answer to your son or daughter if this kid went off and took his own life when you could have saved it?

God is here, whether we ring the doorbell bloody from a fist-fight or we stole the money. The door is open for Jesus' sake; God comforts us and patches us up and pays the money for Jesus' sake. It sounds childish—sure, if we think that love is childish. Happily, God doesn't think so. But we can only get at this mystery through images dealing with love.

Thank you, God, that the way to you is always open through
Jesus Christ.

Mortgaged to the Hilt

Mark 10:45; Rom 13:14; Gal 3:27; Rom 3:24; Rom 5:11; 2 Cor 5:17; Rom 8:16–17; Eph 6:12; Col 1:13

There was talk in the village about one of the small farmers in the vicinity; concerned talk, not unkind. "He's mortgaged to the hilt. Who'll be able to get him out of this mess, only the devil knows!" They looked askance at the pastor, but she wasn't worried about the swear word; she was thinking about how the situation could be used in her sermon—an occupational hazard. Suppose we say that a person is like a house . . . and every time that person does something bad, the bad deed increases the mortgage on the house, until finally the person becomes mortgaged to the limit . . . who would pay off the mortgage? Jesus, of course. And even the very devil would not expect it. Almost as good an image as some of Paul's own, I thought.

To accept this illustration, a person must accept the assumption that lies behind it, the assumption that evil has a claim on anyone who does evil. But that is the assumption behind most images in the Bible that deal with the meaning of the death and resurrection of Jesus. It does no good to try proving or disproving it; we simply must accept it as it is. We know full well that there are things, even in our own actions, that separate us from God. And we also know, from experience, that God can bridge the chasm between us.

It's a little distasteful to me that my lovely new illustration deals so much in economic terms. Especially today, when the

Market is the idol we worship most, with many TV ads every day and whole pages devoted to it in the press. I've thought about what art students would do if as a graduation project they had to portray the Market, like one would depict Virtue, the Motherland, or Justice. It would be a god, of course, one who demands offerings, a modern white-collar Cronus, a god who eats its own children.[31] We can speak of an offering in this way, somewhat figuratively, and not as a bloody altar offering. Blood seems barbaric, primitive, something lying outside the bounds of our imagination, something our civilization has outgrown. But many images of the meaning of Christ's work deal with bloody offerings, especially in the Letter to the Hebrews. The letter—actually more a sermon than a letter—presupposes the Jewish cult offerings and the confidence that they were effective, that the blood from bulls and goats could cleanse a person from sin. But if this seems strange or impossible, then the letter's conclusions become likewise impossible.

Can't we put these images aside and use others? Only a couple times when something really gruesome happened in the world have I felt that blood was necessary. As if God were insufficiently near unless God had also bled, as if we could not accept a lesser gesture from God than an execution. The one who must reconcile us to one another, to our lives, and to God, must have suffered to the extreme; this I recognized. But it is a very long way from that recognition to a metaphysical rationale about what was necessary in the battle between God and Satan.

Are we less able to understand the reality of the cross if we do not understand the ancient offerings? I don't think so; we understand a great deal about the cross. I can let dead symbols be; still, sometimes one or another can suddenly become meaningful. At the end of the 1970s I was to write a Lenten sermon on the text: "give his life a ransom for many." I read Bible commentaries, as well as stories from the Second World War, but I realized that I had no direct connection to words like "ransom" or "hostage," and that probably neither did my congregation. But that same week the first airliner hijacking took place and the text opened up to me.

There are so many symbols, especially in Paul; images for describing the Christian's reality virtually well up from him. To be in Christ or in the Spirit is to be justified—as is to put on Christ. "Put on the Lord Jesus Christ!" he writes to Rome and Galatia. "For as many of you as have been baptized into Christ have put on Christ." Or being redeemed, like a slave; Paul speaks of "the redemption that is in Christ Jesus." Or reconciliation, no longer being an enemy of God: "we even boast in God through our Lord Jesus Christ, through whom we have now received reconciliation." Or something utterly new: "If anyone is in Christ, there is a new creation." The new relationship with God is interpreted by the Spirit: "It is that very Spirit bearing witness with our spirit that we are children of God, and if children, then heirs, heirs of God and joint heirs with Christ—if, in fact, we suffer with him so that we may also be glorified with him."

All images of God's love are in the end so insipid. All logical reasoning about the cosmic conflict is so insufficient, so lame. "For our struggle is not against enemies of blood and flesh, but against the rulers, against the authorities, against the cosmic powers of this present darkness, against the spiritual forces of evil in the heavenly places." How can human language describe this? How can we imagine that human logic can follow God into the fight for our freedom? Yet some images reflect a reality we do know: "He has rescued us from the power of darkness and transferred us into the kingdom of his beloved Son." And that's the truth.

A New Word

Song 5:15–16; 2:8–9; 3:1; 8:6; Isa 6:8

"I love you," says the six-year-old, and the word is born anew, shimmering. We wear out words and no word is so worn out as "love." Sometimes I'd like to create a new word. When something suddenly glows within me, when my heart flip-flops like a northern pike on the bottom of the boat, just when I thought it was dead.

I want to make a new word
for what you do to me
when you see me behind the barriers and behind my fears
I will create a new word
a final, definitive word
from out of the resistant material I'm made of

Like snowmelt dripping from the roof in March
all words for "love" bought or stolen
born yesterday and already cast aside
striking, striking against the stone
without leaving a mark
But against the south wall the crocus breaks through
in its sacred reappearance

There are spaces within us that can only be opened from the outside. There are sides of us that can only be seen in a mirror.

We must dare to love. We must dare to love, even if we risk losing, and then forever after see him in each and every person who looks like him. Even if we search long for him and our heart aches. No one is as beautiful as he. "His appearance is like Lebanon; he is altogether desirable." His movements fill my eyes and become a model for how a man should move. "Look, he comes, leaping upon the mountains, bounding over the hills. My beloved is like a gazelle or a young stag." I conform my body to his; all my life long I lie down to sleep close against him, even when for many years he has no longer been there. "Upon my bed at night I sought him whom my soul loves; I sought him, but found him not." Nothing is as empty as the empty space beside me—and many are they who know what I mean.

There are some people we must stay away from so as not to destroy the life we are living. It grieves us when we see that potential love is rendered impossible by the way things are or by some kind of distance.

> *like a common ground of sorrow*
> *like a farewell a thousand years ago*
> *like a cloud over ravines*
> *like falling though the bottom*
> *like a vault of time*
>
> *like a sorrow beneath the water's surface are your eyes*
> *like a surface that moistens are the tints in your eyes*
> *like the skin of a pike in blue and green are your eyes*
> *like glimpsing a fish in the deep*
> *like a fish of sorrow*

It is a wonderful thing to have been made capable of loving. Nor is there anything so painful. "Love is strong as death; passion fierce as the grave." There is no way to write a book about suffering without writing about love. Whether it is love we had, love we lost, or love we rejected. There is no way to wait for love without pain. There is no way to wait for love without loving. It is by loving that we learn to love.

Is this the greatest thing in life? I can only say so if I may also say that there are many kinds of love, something that has become much clearer to me in later years. Friends, children, books, birds. It has also become much clearer that the days of possessive loving are over.

> *I have been sitting at my desk today trying to study*
> *But all day long your name has been raining down over me from the ceiling*
> *I caught it in my hand and clutched it hard, possessively*
> *until I had almost crushed it to pieces*
> *It was printed with lovely, even, capital letters*
> *and my hair was full of it, like confetti*
> *This evening I'll have to shake it out of my clothes*

Children and calling—or perhaps calling and children—became more important than being a couple. Thank God I was never forced to make a choice. I have indeed had to drop my association with other people, but these two gifts and duties have run in parallel for me.

My identity is tied up in the call. Lord, here I am; send me! It is here that I am, in the sending. But love is like love, and longing is like longing. I am not created to yearn only with my soul. How do I yearn for my beloved? In missing him against the skin of my inner arms, in the absence of his hand under my head as I fall asleep. How do I long for God? In my aching joints, in sleeplessness and all this horror I feel over violence.

> *And in the end, nothing is necessary*
> *nothing other than God*
> *nothing but the love that is a blind confidence in life*

It is no longer necessary, my faith
Not the rock foundation
It is not necessary to stand tall
God is with the sparrow that falls
Only one thing is needed:
daring to fall

Built to Last Forever

Ps 118; Luke 19:37–40; Rev 1:8; Mark 11:9; Matt 21:12–17

He is nearly there. Soon they will cry out, "Blessed is he who comes in the name of the Lord!" That phrase "he who comes" is the oldest of all messianic names, if we can even call it a name. But he acknowledges it and takes the call of being God's Messiah. He accepts the song of praise on the Mount of Olives.

But I'm not on the Mount of Olives with Psalm 118. It is, rather, a psalm for Jerusalem, for the temple, for the one who will call himself "the one who is, who was, and who is to come." There are, obviously, palm branches and nationalism in the shouts around him. But for me, it is primarily a psalm for Västergötland.[32] It is there I experienced it. It lives in me and I in it. It has become God's word to me.

"They surrounded me, surrounded me on every side; in the name of the LORD I cut them off! They surrounded me like bees; they were extinguished like a fire of thorns." It was often like that—even for him. Sneering and polemical attacks could be like poisonous stinging insects, the agony of making a difficult decision like the swelling from a bite. My own bee swarm was in my little brother's beehives on the family's little plot of ground at Kinnekulle,[33] where I sought refuge to think and pray in solitude.

"Out of my distress I called on the LORD; the LORD answered me and set me in a broad place." The spot was not a "broad place" exactly, but there I found freedom from conflicting demands and from those who "pushed me hard, so that I was falling," The silence intensified as I lit a fire in the fireplace and wound up Grandpa's old clock. The dog's nails clicked on the linoleum; stars came out in the night sky. "The LORD helped me; he has become my salvation."

He himself went up into the mountains to be alone and to pray. Could the view he had there have been any better than the one over Lake Vänern, with Läckö Castle[34] shimmering in the sunrise? Is there anywhere more gorgeous than Kinnekulle when the wild cherries are in bloom?

Going further in the psalm takes us across the border into Värmland.[35] Some pastors are buried in a churchyard there, near Lake Vänern, on the west side of the church.[36] One of the markers bears the inscription, "I shall not die, but I shall live, and recount the deeds of the LORD."

It's been the same for me. Time after time life has turned suddenly dangerous, but I survived. Time after time I have *known* that it was impossible go on any longer, to put up with life, or the persecution, or the preaching, and I went to bed fully convinced of it. But then I'd be wakened by the ringing phone, or I'd meet someone or get a letter in the morning mail: "We need you to do this, to write that, to speak. You're the only one who can do it!" Thus the call was renewed, and I "was enticed" into going on, made a promise before I had thought more about it. It always happened like this; no praise or consoling word from God, just a new assignment.

You were not permitted to live, Lord, at least not here on earth. You live another sort of life, hidden with God in heaven. Someone else now must bear witness to your mighty deeds. We do what we can. "Open to me the gates of righteousness, that I may enter through them and give thanks to the LORD." Back to Västergötland, for the gates of righteousness were there on the doors of the little church at Flämslätt, though they aren't especially impressive. It was there that righteousness became clear to me, both the righteousness already sent to us and the righteousness a Christian still awaits. It was here I began to understand the things of God; here the gates were opened in a way they never were at home in Göteborg. "This is the gate of the LORD; the righteous shall enter through it."

That word is printed in the prayer book I bought there in 1960. I think we were celebrating Epiphany[37] at Flämslätt's new church. At a Christian retreat for high school students the year before, we bundled up in all the woolens and boots we had, got on a bus and headed for the church at the ancient Varnhem cloister for morning worship. Faulty heaters under the benches warmed a few backsides, but the living light from the large crown-shaped lamps hanging from the ceiling showed us the Lord's glory. And there is a cornerstone at Varnhem. "The stone that the builders rejected has become the chief cornerstone. This is the LORD's doing; it is marvelous in our eyes."

A cornerstone can be the first stone that builders lay in constructing a house. It is supplied with scorings for lining things up: a level horizontal mark, and at a right angle to it a vertical mark, provided for measuring and making walls plumb. But "cornerstone" can also refer to the keystone, set at the top of an arch, holding it together.

There is an arch in the ruins of Varnhem cloister. Most of the surviving walls are no more than knee high. But at one spot stands an arch, a single course of stones, leading to an open space filled with cowslips and violets and centuries-old masonry. It was likely built for a vaulted room, apparently as a doorway, when the cloister was founded around 1150. Now, however, everything surrounding it has fallen down, and if someone were to knock out its topmost stone, the one bearing the weight of all the others, this arch would instantly collapse in a heap. But the keystone holds it all together, just as it has for the last 850 years. It is obviously not built for time merely, but for eternity. It is wonderful in our eyes.

You, Lord, are the cornerstone holding our church together, even as it falls down around us. This is why I want to join my voice in the hosannas from Mount Olivet, hosannas that ring out wherever the church is gathered. Over and over, wherever I have served, in countless family devotionals at Advent and on Palm Sunday, I have done as the psalm says, with crowds of happy children, all excited and wide-eyed, full of anticipation. "Join in the festal procession with branches, up to the horns of the altar."

Lord, I think you may remain silent now; the children will take up the cry as long as there is a church or sanctuary left. They will be the last to grow silent. And when they do, the very stones will cry out; you yourself promised it. What an appalling cry that will be!

Like a Weaver His Cloth

Isa 38

It is such fun to weave, especially a rag rug, to sit there with the ball of material and think out how to make something beautiful from what I have to work with, from the treasures I have come by. Or to slam the boom to when I feel angry, upset, or frustrated, and to see a truly lovely combination of stripes and colors coming forth just the same. To work with the warp and weft and heddle, with the shuttle and weaving reed—all those wonderful new words that follow in the wake of learning a new handcraft.

I wonder if King Hezekiah did any weaving himself, or if he merely saw it done. He was a contemporary of Isaiah, toward the end of the eighth century B.C., and at that time weaving was done on a frame, like we do on a Laplander's *bandgrind*,[38] only on a larger scale. It was easily portable for a people who were still partly nomadic.

In any case, he had seen a piece of finished fabric cut down from the weaving frame, for he sang about it. At the time, he probably thought he was out of danger, having just escaped an attack of the king of Assyria, escaped in fact without using any weapons. He had done it through diplomacy, and apparently with a little luck, since the Assyrians had found themselves threatened on another front and were forced to pull back their troops. Hezekiah had to forfeit some of his territory, but he had lost none of his people, and not even Jerusalem. He built there the Pool of Siloam with its waterways[39] and purified the temple from dubious images. In other words, he was a good, pious, peaceful king.

But then he grew ill, gravely ill, apparently from an infected wound. Isaiah spoke to him in earnest: "Put your house in order, because you are about to die." In a situation like that, a person can experience great fear, whether fear of whatever comes after death, or fear of helplessness and the dying process—in Hezekiah's case, pain, fever, and possibly gangrene. Or a deep calm can fall upon a person instead, because soon the voice will be heard that says it is time now to lay down life's tools and to go empty-handed to the Lord. Or again, one can be overcome with worry, especially when the children are still small: "How will they get along when I am gone?"

Hezekiah believed just as his culture did, that there was nothing to look forward to beyond death, or possibly nothing more than a shadow-land. He isn't afraid, but he is angry and upset. He turns his face to the wall and prays. He believes that God is just, that when someone has been as good a person as Hezekiah has been, he ought to get something out of it—and it should happen now in this present life. But it is not in that sense that God is just, calculating plusses and minuses and equally doling out light and darkness. God is righteous and loves what is just, but above all God is compassionate—warmhearted and generous, as we might say if we were speaking of a human being. God lets Hezekiah live, promising him another fifteen years. Isaiah puts a fig cake on Hezekiah's wound and it heals up.[40] Then Hezekiah composes a wonderful song.

With a voice of weeping, like the plaintive call of a dove or the shrill cry of the swallow, he expresses his sorrow that he will never again see human beings. He finds images for death that speak even to me, still after all this time. "My dwelling is plucked up and removed from me like a shepherd's tent." Exactly. One day it will be no more. This tent that I now live in needs only to be removed from me in order to return to dust—and that doesn't frighten me.

"I have woven my life to its end, like a weaver his cloth, and he cuts me off from the loom." Right! One day it will be so. And of course all who, like Hezekiah, have cut down a weaving from the loom know that we cannot properly see the design in the rug *until* we take it down. Only then will we see where we have made mistakes and been careless. Then we'll be reminded of the various darker and lighter parts of the pattern—the blue of torn work clothes, the old black mourning coat, the colorful child's dress, a white curtain in the sunshine.

But I believe there is a pattern in every fabric. I believe that God weaves with us throughout our lives, weaves in his design even though we will not be able to see it until the finished cloth is rolled out. It is the pattern of reconciliation, a cross. No matter how we do our weaving, that pattern always shows up too, and the whole effect is beautiful, and God is compassionate and full of grace.

I Am Hard Pressed between the Two

Phil 1:21–24; 2 Cor 5:2–4; 2 Cor 4:16–17; 2 Pet 3:13

How glorious the earth![41]—and how appalling, and everything in between. Just now, every park and garden in Lund is in full glory, yellow with winter aconite, white with snowdrops, radiantly blue with Siberian squill. The first crocuses are coming up along the south wall of the greenhouse in Lund's Botanical Gardens. My grandchild checks to see if one of them has opened up and wants to know if it might possibly be a cousin of the crocus with the saffron on its pistils.

"Promise me you'll teach me everything!" Yes, my dear child, I'll keep doing my best. It's a good reason to go on living.

Still, I can just as easily find myself longing for heaven, longing for death. It can strike me at any particular time, whether happy or difficult, like a breath of warm wind. It doesn't mean anything; it's harmless. It's merely a reminder that I am here in time and earthly space. Eternity embraces everything round about me, and my longing blows upon me like a breeze from that same eternity.

Many Christians experience this. "I am hard pressed between the two," says Paul, very appropriately, in his letter to the Philippians, where he debates with himself whether he wants to live or to die. Clearly he, if anyone, can experience the longing to escape. He's had a rough time of it and has worked hard; he's bothered by an illness he cannot seem to shake off. This longing to escape can be just that, a desire to be done with a difficult life.

Paul has another longing: the Lord Jesus. He finds himself divided, sitting in a prison somewhere, knowing that he could soon be put to death, yet hoping to survive and be set free. "For to me, living is Christ and dying is gain," he writes. "If I am to live in the flesh, that means fruitful labor for me; and I do not know which I prefer. I am hard pressed between the two: my desire is to depart and be with Christ, for that is far better; but to remain in the flesh is more necessary for you."

Someone needs him, and so he wants to go on living. Yes, it can be that way; we know how it feels, especially when there are children involved. But I just wonder how much Paul needed to be needed. To what extent was he actually able to live in obscurity? How unnoticed can our work be, how much insignificance can we endure, and still find what we do to be worth doing?

I don't think anyone could have wanted less from life than did an old pastor I met in a nursing home. He told me about his work of intercessory prayer. There are so many people one can speak to God about when almost the only thing one can do is to lie flat on one's back! But of course the day eventually came when he could no longer even pray, when his mind couldn't keep thoughts and people together. I was angry and upset about it, imagining that he was in despair, and I sought the right words to say to him. But he smiled: "Now I am just someone they can practice their love on."

For my part, I don't think it would be enough to keep me going even if many people needed me. I am so shriveled up all winter long that I am unable to be there for anyone and can scarcely keep up my own spirits. Could I not request something for myself too, something to make *me* happy? What do you think, Paul? Quite frankly, there are times when we have to go on living simply as an act of sheer obedience, almost as when we keep on praying even though doing so has long since begun to seem pointless, both to us and to God.

Paul is fed up with his body. He doesn't even want to bother with going though death; he'd rather skip straight out of his tattered, sick, and weary carcass and directly into glory. He'd prefer to dispense with what we all dread, that process of the so-called "putting off." It often consists of what is very "bodily" indeed: aphasia, dementia, incontinence, and other things we regard as completely undeserved.

Paul survives, however, and we do not know what sort of death and final days God determined for him—nor what sort God determines for us. Paul writes to Corinth: "So we do not lose heart. Even though our outer nature is wasting away, our inner nature is being renewed day by day. For this slight momentary affliction is preparing us for an eternal weight of glory beyond all measure."

For us, just as for Paul, longing can be a longing for God, since we do have an inkling of what it will be like at home with God. Then shall all evil be done with, all my pain, my agony, my doublemindedness, my weeping and fatigue, my loneliness. Then I'll be done with hearing about animals being exterminated, about boys who kill each other, whether in battle by order of generals or on the school grounds by their own initiative. We pray in worship services that God would soon bring forth the day of the new heavens and the new earth, where righteousness dwells! It is a prayer that goes to the depth of all our souls.

And when at last we do get to heaven, then all our masks will have fallen away, all sham, all the roles we've learned to enforce on genders, groups, and cultures. When death finally puts an end to all limitations and every wall falls before the victorious onslaught of simplicity, then we shall be able to see each other face to face, such as we finally will be. Then we shall we see the Lord face to face, such as he is, always and forever. That will be lovely beyond imagination.

Another note vibrates within me, something like a sense of the unreality in everything earthly. At times, so-called reality is so ephemeral that I can keep my grip on it only with difficulty, so transparent that I can scarcely keep myself here. Often it would be the easiest thing in the world simply to let go.

So easy to step over the threshold
so easy to cross to the other side
Not even a guarded door
no dark waters
only a torn curtain at the boundary
Someone slashed it with his sword
and immediately there came out blood and water
Through the rent the light of the Unheard Of

So easy to take this small step
So insubstantial everything on this side

One Who Knows What It Is to Lose Someone

John 11:1–16; John 14:1–7; John 20:19–29

We run into Thomas rather frequently in John's Gospel; three times John actually has Thomas speak.

Safe on the other side of the Jordan River, Jesus gets word that his friend Lazarus is sick; Lazarus is a brother of a pair of women who were very close to Jesus. Jesus delays. He is in danger, wanted by the police, which is why he is out of the country. He knows that he is about to be killed, but he knows it will happen in Jerusalem and that it will happen at Passover. When the time is right, he must go. His disciples try to advise him.

> *"They wanted to stone you, you know! They're after your life! Stay here!"*

But now he's made up his mind. The appointed time has come. And Thomas speaks, his words falling heavily, like stones:

> *"Let us also go, that we may die with him."*

He sounds like a person who knows what it is to lose someone. "Not again! I can't take it! I won't go through it!"

He's called Didymos; that is, the Twin. Thomas the Twin. Where is the other twin? We will never know. He doesn't show up in the Jesus story. Perhaps he is dead. Maybe he died at birth and is there only as a shadow, an empty hole, a memory of that space where nothing exists but nearness, touch, and togetherness. Perhaps he died later on, and the parting was not like two people losing hold of each another's hands; it was more like if I were to clasp another's hand in mine and then chop them both off, so that something of me remains with that other person and something of him is always with me, and the wound bleeds a long time and is easily reopened.

Perhaps at one time Thomas wasn't just one of a twosome, but half of a single, united entity. Perhaps now he had found a similar oneness again, a healing, a love, a sense of belonging, something new to be part of. In that case he would likely feel it is easier to die than to go through this amputation all over again. If Jesus dies, why should I go on living? Better to be where the beloved is, even if it is in death and darkness and hell.

Some days later Jesus makes one final attempt to explain and forewarn. The feast is over. Judas has gone out. It is night. Jesus talks and talks, calming them, comforting them. "Do not be troubled! I am going away and I will come again. I go to prepare a place for you with my Father and your Father. You know the way."

They respond with confusion and despair. Once more it is Thomas who speaks, as if he were the least comforted in the little flock. He is the one who simply must know, who hangs on tight. Momma, where are you going? When will you come back? You are coming back, aren't you? What will we do if we have trouble? Who will help us? "Lord, we do not know where you are going. How can we know the way?"

Did Thomas learn anything just now from hearing Jesus say that he himself is the way? He goes to the cross, yes, but what kind of way is that? He *goes* a way and he *is* a way. Where's the logic in that? What kind of comfort is this for one who does not want to lose again, for one who doesn't want roads or resting places, but a dwelling place?

And now come the dark days when cowardice and the instinct for self-preservation scatter them into that darkness. When shame and terror make them lock their doors, when the love and courage of the women goes farther than theirs and they hear wondrous rumors. When they continually mull over what they've lost, when they cast blame on each other, when they shriek with pain, when they can weep no more and realize that all their future plans have died with him. What are we going to do now? What's left? Where is God? Where is there a life worth living?

Then suddenly Jesus is standing among them and showing them his poor hands. Joy slowly fills them, trickling into them like a thawed spring brook, growing into a river that overflows its banks. His face is light and it lights up theirs.

But Thomas is not among them when Jesus comes. He doesn't believe them, when they tell him. Is it because he cannot, or because he does not want to? Perhaps it sounds just too good to be true. He hasn't got it in him to hope one more time, only to be disappointed yet again.

> *"Don't give me any more of this talk. I want something more concrete, more tangible. A wound! That's something I'd recognize. A nail and a sword! That's something I know something about!"*

And so he was granted the grace to be overpowered, denied the possibility of escape. He was given a shared fate, a common cup to drink from. A living master to fall down before.

> *"My Lord and my God!"*

Blessed Is He Who Comes

A cross is wedged into my body
among the vertebrae and gristle.
Arched up like a bow
I form a bridge
between emptiness and meaning.

Good Friday stretches out into years.

I keep binding life's tatters
about my body, as it wastes away.
Or is it you, Lord?
Is it you holding me together
between death and life?

Somewhere among these agonies I have my answer.

The Cross
(2 Cor 4:16)

The Donkey King and His Prophets

John 12:12–16; Zech 9:9; Zeph 3:14–15; Ps 118:24–26; Jer 7:1–15;
Isa 56:1–8; Mark 11:15–19

He stands on the Mount of Olives, and the city gleams like gold in the light of the sunrise. There is no more beautiful city than Jerusalem at dawn. He sends for a donkey.

Prophets follow in his train, practically treading on his heels. Right through the midst of the crowds, among confused disciples and people with overheated expectations, they make their way. In fact, they are dancing. Of course they dance; any prophet dances who sees that he has at last been proved right.

Zechariah urges them on, invisible to be sure, but fully audible to anyone who can read the writing and interpret the signs. "Rejoice greatly, O daughter Zion! Shout aloud, O daughter Jerusalem! Lo, your king comes to you; triumphant and victorious is he, humble and riding on a donkey, on a colt, the foal of a donkey."

Zephaniah interrupts him, and at last, after all this time, the people respond. They have been waiting for this for some six hundred years. They dance, too, with light steps (as in Anitra's dance[42]): *Now, now, now he has come!* "Sing aloud, O daughter Zion; shout, O Israel! Rejoice and exult with all your heart, O daughter Jerusalem! The king of Israel, the LORD, is in your midst; you shall fear disaster no more."

And the people answer, *Yes!* Perhaps they see the prophets out of the corners of their eyes; perhaps they sense them in the flapping of a cloak or in a puff of wind. Yes! "This is the day that the

LORD has made; let us rejoice and be glad in it. Save us, we beseech you, O LORD! O LORD, we beseech you, give us success! Blessed is the one who comes in the name of the LORD."

Song, dance, and jubilation; down from the mountain they come, across the Kidron Valley and through the Golden Gate, up to the temple. One of the entourage stops. He has never been here before; the brilliance of the scene takes his breath away. But Jesus leaves the donkey and walks on into the temple precincts. Zechariah and Zephaniah remain outside, satisfied. Maybe they, too, gape at Herod's palace and at this temple, a magnificent edifice that will barely be completed before it is destroyed.

Other prophets following him with a heavier step (as in the Hall of the Mountain King[43]) catch up now. Here is Jeremiah, tormented as always, though determined that no one will go lost if he can do something about it, that no sin will escape exposure as long as he can speak. He stands in the gate, and he remembers. For this word once came to Jeremiah from the Lord: "Stand in the gate of the LORD's house, and proclaim there this word: 'Hear the word of the LORD, all you people of Judah, you that enter these gates to worship the LORD. Thus says the LORD of hosts, the God of Israel: Amend your ways and your doings, and let me dwell with you in this place. Do not trust in deceptive words and say, "This is the temple of the LORD, the temple of the LORD, the temple of the LORD!" For if you truly amend your ways and your doings, if you truly act justly one with another . . .'"

But how are they to amend their ways? They can do it simply by practicing what the prophets have always demanded: ordinary, everyday goodness. "If you do not oppress the alien, the orphan, and the widow, or shed innocent blood in this place, and if you do not go after other gods to your own hurt, then I will dwell with you in this place, in the land that I gave of old to your ancestors forever and ever."

Jesus looks around, a wild look in his eye, just as if Jeremiah has coached him. Within the Court of the Gentiles he sees the tables of the moneychangers and the stalls where poor and rich can buy animals for their sacrificial offerings. He grabs a rope and swings it powerfully over his head. The tables are easily knocked over; coins scatter, rolling in every direction, and doves fly upward. He cries out, and Jeremiah cries out with him, "Has this house, which is called by my name, become a den of robbers in your sight? So it is also in my eyes, says the LORD!" Now Isaiah comes to his side, wise with age and suffering, compassionate from all the misery he has seen humanity suffer. He brings promises; he offers an alternative: Unless . . . unless God's own people want their God, room will be found for others.

> *"Do not let the foreigner joined to the LORD say, 'The LORD will surely separate me from his people'; and do not let the eunuch say, 'I am just a dry tree.' For thus says the LORD: To the eunuchs who keep my sabbaths, who choose the things that please me and hold fast my covenant, I will give, in my house and within my walls, a monument and a name better than sons and daughters.*
>
> *"And the foreigners who join themselves to the LORD, to minister to him, to love the name of the LORD, and to be his servants, all who keep the sabbath, and do not profane it, and hold fast my covenant, these I will bring to my holy mountain, and make them joyful in my house of prayer."*

Both Isaiah and Jesus call out a message from God: "My house shall be called a house of prayer for all peoples." Jesus has announced a clarification of his program. He is the king of the poor; he is God who lives among his people. He repeats God's permanent demand for goodness, and if they will not hear it . . . well, then there are others waiting.

In the Temple Precincts

Mark 12:13–17; Mark 12:18–27; Luke 11:27–28; Mark 11:27–33;
Mark 12:1–12; Isa 5:1–7; Matt 21:28–32; Matt 23:4; Matt 23:27;
Matt 23:37; Luke 12:35–37; Matt 22:1–13; Heb 13:12–13

He's now been standing in the temple precincts for three days,
maybe four, arguing with his opponents. He can be sharp-tongued.
Many of them would like to trap him in his words. It is a lot like an
election campaign. Just like us, he lives in a pluralistic world with
numerous political parties.

The Zealots, who clamor for violence and rebellion, were disappointed last Sunday. The Pharisees, who observe the law in the mi-
nutest detail—he is most like them, and it is with them he wrangles
most—for he wants genuine goodness and not just a bunch of
Bible-thumpers. Here they come again, full of flattery, at least to
begin with. "We know that you make no distinctions among people
and that you bow to no one if you think you are right. So tell us,
should we pay tax to Caesar?"

Clever question! If he answers yes, he sets himself against all
those who want no worldly authority over them at all—other than
a Jewish one, perhaps. If he answers no, he of course commits rebellion against the occupation powers. He asks for a coin.

"Whose image is this?" he says when they hand him a denarius.

"Caesar's."

"Well, then, give to Caesar what belongs to Caesar and to God what belongs to God."

The Sadducees spin out an appalling story. "A man married and then died childless, and his brother had to marry his widow." That was in fact the law. A woman was inherited just like one of the livestock. Indeed this poor woman was inherited by six successive brothers before she finally died.

"Who will she be married to in heaven?" they ask. If the law is valid—and in their view it was unconditionally so—then in that case the whole question of heaven becomes absurd, which is exactly what they thought of it.

"She won't be married to anyone," says Jesus. "People aren't married off like that in heaven." In heaven, people aren't treated like mere animals or things; they aren't married off or sold or exploited. No one is just a wife or a unit of manpower or a consumer or a caretaker. In heaven, each and every person has a personal identity; each one is seen and loved by God.

It reminds us of something he said on an earlier occasion. A woman came forward from the crowd when he was healing the sick. She cried out:

"Blessed is she who bore you in her womb and nursed you!"

"Quite the contrary," he said. "Blessed is the one who hears the word of God and obeys it."

It's not because you are married to someone, not because of any status or titles you have, or because of your impressive relatives or your fame, not even because you are the mother of Jesus, that you are called blessed and belong to the kingdom. In heaven—both the heaven that begins here and now and the one yet to come—it is your own identity that counts, and your own relationship to God.

In heaven each person is the apple of God's eye and a person in her own right.

> *"What authority do you have for saying this?" The question comes from those with religious clout, and he turns it back to them: "What did the Baptist have as his authority?" But they can't answer him, and so he refuses to continue the conversation.*

He stops now for a while, but comes back later to ask some questions of his own. Like every conscientious preacher, he casts around for images and illustrations that will make it easy for the head to understand and difficult for the heart to avoid.

> *"A man planted a vineyard, just like God did in Isaiah's time. And the renters killed the man's envoys and even his son. What will happen to these renters?"*

The question is painfully simple to answer—but he is met with silence.

> *"A man had two children. One of them said yes when the father asked him to help out with the work, but he did nothing. The other said no, but then went out and worked anyway. Which one does God want? What sort of person does God want?"*

He vacillates between pronouncing woe on them and simply weeping over them.

> *"You that bind up heavy burdens . . . you who are whitewashed outside like tombs and are rotten inside . . . you hypocrites . . . why do you not want me . . . I truly want you, I wanted to gather you to me like a hen gathers her chicks . . ."*

The tone of things becomes more desperate. Parable after parable unfolds toward judgment, death, and the great messianic feast. "At the end of time, for time shall indeed come to an end," he says.

"Your time, my time, the world's time." Then he shall be visible to all and recognized by all. Then it will no longer be possible to escape him. One day will truly be the final day.

> *"Be dressed for action!" he says to them about that day.*[44]

This can mean to get ready to travel, be always ready to move out. Reconciled perhaps, with God and with other people.

> *"Be dressed for action!"*

It's also what those who work hard must do, those who reap the harvest or care for the sick, or who wait tables. This readiness to serve is so important in fact, that Jesus says that he himself will practice it even in heaven. He says:

> *"When you come home to me for the feast, I will dress myself for action"*—in plain English: *"I will put on my apron"*—*"and I'll serve you at your table."*

It will be a wedding! Oh how glorious! Everyone is invited, first of course the obvious ones, who actually don't come. Oh woe to them! But then the outcasts are invited, and the poor, the sick, and the unemployed on the street corners, those who have ended up in the gutter. They are being led by the hand, supported on the arm of a strong and healthy man, right into the feast. Oh what joy!

But one day the door is closed. It's possible to come too late. It's possible to end up outside. There truly is an "outside." There is darkness and weeping and a nightmare one never wakes from. There is no escaping the fact that this is what he has been saying, over and over.

> *"But what about me?" said one of my confirmation students as we were reading this text. "What will happen to me? I'm always late for everything!" While the pastor groped about for something to say, one of the*

other students answered confidently. "If you come too late, Jesus will be sitting on the porch waiting for you."

Exactly. There is darkness, weeping, a hell, an outside. We cannot get around the fact that he said so. But neither can we escape the fact that the cross is being raised up out there, outside the walls. That is where he will now soon go, outside, to knock the walls down.

Who Is He Looking For?

Mark 12:41–44; 2 Cor 8:1–5; Mark 14:3–9

What sort of person does he want? Who is he looking for these days? It's not easy to say exactly, but in the midst of all these words, speeches, and parables there is someone who acts quietly. And when all the talking is done, there is yet another person there. Perhaps they can show us something that cannot be put into words.

He sits down for a while outside the Court of Women at the temple and from his seat he can watch how people put money into the offering boxes. Many of the wealthy were giving a good deal. Then a poor widow comes along and gives what she has, nothing but a few pennies. Yet he calls to his disciples and points her out to them.

"She gave most of all. She gave everything she had to live on, everything she possessed in her poverty."

So thoughtlessly irresponsible! How would she manage now? Shouldn't we always keep back a little, take thought for tomorrow? That is clearly not his opinion of the matter.

Nor was it the attitude among the congregations in Macedonia, the ones Paul boasts of in his second letter to Corinth: "They voluntarily gave according to their means, and even beyond their means . . . they gave themselves first to the Lord and, by the will of God, to us."

"Pay attention to her," says Jesus, "to her who exceeds her means, who in fact first gives herself."

And that very evening, or perhaps the next, there is another woman, also nameless, and he has this to say about her:

Don't forget her! She gave everything she had. "She has performed a good service for me. . . . Wherever the good news is proclaimed in the whole world, what she has done will be told in remembrance of her."

I can easily imagine the scene, as if I had been there.

A figure stood in the doorway, still and heavy. She looked as if she needed to catch her breath a bit. Or let her eyes grow accustomed to the dim light from the oil lamps fluttering in the draft. Someone turned to tell her to shut the door, but clamped up. She was obviously not the sort of person you simply told to do this or that. She was a woman who does what she has to do, sometimes because she's been sent to do it, sometimes just because it's time it was done.

And that's exactly how she looked. Not at all a young woman, but one who had already raised sons and daughters, and perhaps grandchildren who could often bring a little smile to her stern mouth. Her hair, still thick, was gathered in a grey braid over one shoulder.

A midwife, that's how she looked. Or perhaps something even more intimidating. She looked like the sort of woman who insists that umbilical cords are cut correctly, that brides are properly dressed, that corpses are washed like they should be washed. Not the kind of woman you tell to shut the door behind her.

But she shut it now just the same, because her eye had clearly fallen on the one she was looking for. She stepped forward and positioned herself behind him. Jesus looked up at her and smiled slightly as if he recognized her, though I can swear to it that none of the rest of us had ever seen her before. She was not a woman you'd easily forget, I can tell you.

She pulled something out of the bag hanging from her belt, a small flask, and with a powerful snap she broke the neck off. Immediately a wonderful fragrance spread throughout Simon's tidy, pedantic, boring little house. A fragrance that mingled with the smoke from the fire, with the sweat and dust from those of us who had been walking all day, and with that peculiar scent of fear that had been following us for a long time, picked up for several days now by the dogs in every village we passed through.

Now the woman lifted her strong brown hands and poured the oil into his hair while she slowly and quietly recited some sort of blessing. Jesus looked up at her again and nodded. She had done what she had to do. She let her gaze glide over us all again, as if she were evaluating us, and it wasn't all that certain that we passed the test. Then she left us in our confusion.

A king had been crowned, that was clear enough. The scent of nard was the scent of wealth and power, of the court, velvet, and gold, of whisperings and intrigues, of victories and triumphs. A son of David had been installed in his office.

A dying man had been anointed. The scent was the scent of earth and decay and autumn, right there in the midst of the preparations for Passover. Such a perversion. The wind of fear blew through the room again.

And confusion broke out in aggression . . .

God's Kingdom Is Near

Mark 1:14–15; Mark 13:3–37; Mark 14:61–62; Dan 7:13; Dan 3:16–25

This is now the third year he's been preaching about the kingdom of God. "Now after John was arrested, Jesus came to Galilee, proclaiming the good news of God."

"The time is fulfilled, and the kingdom of God has come near; repent, and believe in the good news."

That's what his first sermon sounded like, nothing more than that. There is brightness about it, like youthful enthusiasm on a sunny day. The burden of John's fate doubtless lay heavy upon Jesus, and he knew that he must now do what he was sent to do. And he did not know how much time he had for doing it. Yet these few short sentences vibrate with joy. What is he actually saying?

God's kingdom has come because I have come. You receive God's kingdom when you receive me. There is no other to be found, anywhere; yet it is right here, near you. The time is short, as always. Swedish educator and women's activist Honorine Hermelin (1886–1977) penned the following lines:

Today
seeds must be sown
for tomorrow it will rain
today the harvest must be gathered in

for tomorrow comes the frost
today the dam must be built
for tomorrow the river has dropped[45]
today I will write my last will and testament
for tomorrow I die

This is exactly how every reformer with clear and open eyes realizes that the time is short, perpetually short. What must be done must be done today.

Thus his tone has become more desperate now in Jerusalem. The last things he says, perhaps just to a small circle of friends, deal with the last things that will take place—in time. Then it's time for something else. And this last thing is frightening, strange. He urges them not be frightened when they hear cries of alarm and rumors of war, for that is merely the beginning of birth pains— those pains that mean that something new is about to be born.

But how can we *not* be frightened? How are we to remain calm? "They will hand you over to councils; and you will be beaten . . . brother will betray brother to death . . . you will be hated by all because of my name . . . woe to those who are pregnant and to those who are nursing infants in those days . . . for in those days there will be suffering, such as has not been from the beginning of the creation that God created until now, no, and never will be. . . ."

It's a little worrying, all this talk of suffering. Fortunately, it's not some kind of glorification of suffering, and we are reminded of the prayer, "Lead us not into temptation!" Perhaps this thing he is speaking of is the final great testing, the last great risk of failing to hold on fast to God. Pray to be spared from it. He himself would have to go through it just a day or so later.

But he continues, now bringing all of creation into it. We are in the same boat with stars and suns, trees and earth, caught in a wave of events. "But in those days, after that suffering, the sun will be darkened, and the moon will not give its light, and the stars will be falling from heaven, and the powers in the heavens will be shaken."

All these visions of destruction—visions we know the first century was full of—seem strange to us, yet they are also frighteningly familiar. We can recognize ourselves in each and every description; all of it has happened before and all of it is happening now. We on the earth have had only four days—*four days!*—of worldwide peace since 1945. And we scarcely need to be reminded of all the devilishly cruel things we human beings do to one another.

The apocalyptic visions of the first century refer to this escalation of catastrophes we recognize; they refer as well to the Day of the Lord, when evil will be uprooted and God's people rescued. The prophets concur and one of them speaks of a mysterious son of man. Now Jesus takes up that title himself. "Then they will see 'the Son of Man coming in clouds' with great power and glory, and he will gather his elect from the ends of the earth to the ends of heaven."

Why does he bring this up precisely at this point, right here, right now? It must be incredibly important for him if he decides to spend his very last days on it. His final sermon has a darkness hanging over it, a menacing fear.

But that final darkness and the first light have the same center. "God's kingdom is near," he had said, "because I am here." He makes use of contemporary concepts, but at the same time he corrects them.

> *"This is how it is," he says. "All this shall take place! Yet it all has to do with me! Everything shall be summed up in me, all things in heaven and all things on the earth. Then God's kingdom shall come in its glory, with great distress. But when the Kingdom comes, it is I who come. And for that reason, you must not be afraid!*

But even he who says this doesn't know when it will happen. He remains limited in his humanity. "But about that day or hour no one knows, neither the angels in heaven, nor the Son, but only the Father."

It's so strange. He who one day will judge the world does not know when it will be, so deep is his immersion in humanity. Yet he identifies himself as the Son of man. What did his friends think he meant?

Standing before the high priest, he was perfectly understood; his claim was comprehended in all its fullness.

"Are you the Messiah, the Son of the Blessed One?"

"I am; and 'you will see the Son of Man seated at the right hand of the Power,' and 'coming with the clouds of heaven.'"

This understanding led to his death.

Are we afraid? The entire transformation we look forward to is stamped with his example, the example of the grain of wheat. He who comes in the skies of heaven is portended by Joseph, thrown into the well, by Daniel, keeping watch all night in the den of lions, by Jonah in the belly of the fish, and by the men cast into the fiery furnace.

Are we afraid? Isn't there a fourth person right there among us in the burning heat of that oven?

He Comes the Same Day You Do

Matt 26:14–16; Matt 26:47–50; Matt 27:3–5

I suppose we should follow you now, Judas. We just can't understand why you took the path you took. In picture after picture there you are, a shadow over you as you slink away from the festivities, purse in hand, ugly, dark, crouching, threatening.

Then the next scene. You thrust your chin out like an ape and kiss him in the darkness of the garden. The light falls upon the disgusting deed—light from the torches in the soldiers' hands.

It wasn't as simple as a matter of money. We can likely rule that out as slander. What was it then? What could have happened to lead you to make a choice like this?

Or was it quite simple after all? Was it the sort of thing we all experience, a single destructive trait, a small act committed in the heat of anger or the drought of apathy? A small act that became larger than we intended it to be, that had unforeseen consequences?

I don't know. I do know, however, that I want to scream at him. But I also want to scream at everyone who minimizes such things, who doesn't recognize the little evil deed that destroys a relationship of love, who trivializes what crosses the line, wherever the line is.

"What in the hell are you doing, Judas?
Are you betraying your Lord
and selling him for a fat reward?"

"No, my price is cheap
for betrayed trust
and for love gone lost
The price of a slave
and the price for my lord
thirty silver pieces in my hand
and on the floor at their feet
the feet of those whose mouths laugh with scorn
whose backs are straight with confidence and satisfaction"

If you've ever known what it is to go too far, if you've ever once said an unkind word that made the warmth fade from someone's eyes, if you ever struck a child and broke her trust, if you ever betrayed another's deepest secret—then Judas himself must be allowed to scream at you.

"Why have you abandoned me?
Look at me, whoever you are,
here with the rope around my neck
my eyes turn toward the silence
and I cry, to hell with you all!"

Do we see him? Him who kissed the one whom he followed, the one to whom he promised allegiance? How easily a kiss became the sign of treachery. Do we want to know where he was and where he went? Or is it too unpleasant to think about?

"Is hell new for you, Iscariot?"

"No, I am so well acquainted with this place
it is already a familiar land to me
the soul's fall into the realm of terror
My cry freezes up through broken time
Suns shine from a distance of dark-years
for those with solid ground beneath their feet

Who has solid ground underfoot on such a night as this? Who is not afraid of finally one day falling in a bottomless well, forever and ever, into darkest darkness?

Someone must rescue us.
Someone has rescued us.
Someone who cried out in abandonment
so that darkest darkness fell upon the earth.
Someone must speak to Judas in the darkness.
In hell, the ultimate outer place.

"Gone down to hell
has he too, your Lord
Hear him knocking
he wants in and calls out
with blood on his face
'Why have you forsaken me?'"

It's Him, Judas Iscariot!
He comes the same day you do
and through the same darkness
and the same betrayed love
and hell's gates
shall not overcome him

Nameless Nights

Mark 14:18, 44, 56, 65, 71; Mark 15:1, 15, 17, 19

Nights do not have names, strangely enough. So much happens at night. So many babies are born in the night; so many people die before the dawn. Out in the night, mysterious things move about on silent paws, hooves, and wings—things we seldom see, but that are simply there and that watch us without revealing themselves. It is at night that the Queen of the Night[46] blooms and the torturers bring out the tools of their trade. It is at night that he comes whom I long for so much, that love's hot or bitter accusations pour out when disappointment strikes. It is at night that restlessness creeps over those who cannot sleep, and we lie there as if tied to the rails in a tunnel, the train thundering ever nearer. But nights have no names.

This night, a night between Thursday and Friday in April of the year 32, is not a night that can be studied in isolation. It is not a simple matter of him and his final night, a night when he got no sleep. Other images and other texts have been laid over it, resulting in confusion and misconceptions. On my desk there is a newspaper, a journal from Amnesty, a biography about a rich man's wife, a book on the First World War, and a detective novel. They'll do as parallel examples, but you can find others yourself.

Mark tells the story:
"One of you will betray me."

"I am deeply grieved, even to death."
"The one I will kiss is the man."
Many gave false testimony against him.
Some began to spit on him.
"I do not know this man."
They bound Jesus, led him away, and handed him over.
After flogging Jesus, he handed him over to be crucified.

And they clothed him in a purple cloak; and after twisting some thorns into a crown, they put it on him.

They struck his head with a reed and spat upon him.

It sounds so believable. We have heard all this before; much of it we have either been along in or done ourselves. Or we have failed to interfere when we've seen someone doing such things to another person.

Still, there is perhaps something different about this situation. This man was incapable of lying, even in the form of self-deception. He could not blame someone else or appeal to his special circumstances. He could not help but see right through all illusions and all the masks people wear. He was compelled to see everything just as it really was, wickedness and horror, opportunism and cowardice, indifference and impotence. The miracle is that it filled him with compassion and prayer: "Father, forgive them!"

And yet, this part of the story is so easy to believe. We have heard it repeated so often. Some day the smitten one will be able to assert his dignity. Some day the thorns will also be barbed wire.

One night in Jerusalem God was a human being, smitten and spat upon, and he did not retaliate. Thousands of lambs en route to the temple square bleated in anxious fright, soldiers swore, the Sanhedrin met in an uproar, decision-makers were wakened unceremoniously. But in the midst of the noise, the beating and blood, and the power-struggles, there was a quiet place, the eye of the storm, a peace, a premonition of reconciliation, when he made no answer to those who accused him.

A nameless night yielded a promise of dawn.

The Sign of Jonah

It's all so close, so easy to imagine, as if I were there at the gates of Hades with Mary, his mother.

This nightingale is going to drive me mad. Obviously, it intends to sing all night long, even though the warmth of spring air comes only in brief gusts and the clouds fly dark over the full moon's deathly face. It suits me fine: the cold and the wind, a dead moon—but not the smell of fresh grass or a bird that sings incessantly.

Something also smells of myrrh. It must be the empty casks we brought back from the tomb. Mary has always said that it held a special horror for her, the aroma of myrrh, ever since he was a little boy. I've often thought that the whole thing was just a bit exaggerated, that her story of the foreign princes sounded a little odd, not altogether true. A slaughter of children and a flight into exile have a more believable ring to them, since great lords need hardly any reason at all for such abuses, and many have committed them. But I noticed how she flinched when the cask was opened, how wide her eyes grew.

It's been a long and difficult day. We kept as close as we could from the moment they led him out into the street with the crossbeam bound to his shoulders. He was tired and beaten, and looked it. Mary, so long a stranger to his spirit and his soul, made an attempt to rush to his side. Fortunately, an old woman moves slowly and there were many people, so she was hindered.

But when he died, there weren't many of us, and she was able to get near. She took his body into her arms, though only for a few minutes, since a strong sense of fear and impatience pervaded the scene. Still, there was something far off in her eyes, far off, something that kept them from hurrying her. I do not know what it was she saw. She ran her eyes over every part of him, as if she were recognizing again the body she bore in her own, the small child's body she carried on her shoulders as he giggled and laughed, or held in her arms when he cried. She lifted one of his hands and ran her fingers over it, not over the new wounds, but over a thin white scar on his wrist, an old one—perhaps the first one he ever got. Then she sighed and let them take him from her.

The nightingale sings like an idiot. Never again will I be able to hear a nightingale without thinking of this night. I wonder if you are sleeping, Mary. I wonder if you feel the weight in your body as you did those final weeks, as you felt it on the journey just before his birth. I wonder if you feel the weight of his corpse, heavy and limp like a sleeping child. But without a child's warmth and satisfaction when you lift it from where it fell asleep and lay it down in its own bed, and it sighs briefly, snuggles under the covers, and smiles a little in its dreams. Here, however, no one smiled. Sighing and weeping aplenty, though subdued and with anxious glancing in every direction. And already his body began to grow cold.

There is a chill and darkness in the tomb now, Mary. Is that what you are thinking about as you sigh, tossing and turning on your bed? Yet one thing is over now, Mary. The anxiety you felt from the myrrh that first day is over and done. Now you know where he was headed. The night is dark indeed, but no darker than a mother's womb. The nightingale sings in the night, and this night will not give birth. But tomorrow night shall open its womb at dawn.

Something tells me this, something he said about the sign of Jonah. The tomb is cold indeed, but no colder than the belly of the great fish. On the third day, the cold shall cast him up onto the shore in a wave of fire.

We wanted a sign. We wanted marvels. We did not want blood and pain, cold and darkness. You shall have no sign, he said. You will receive no other sign than the sign of Jonah.

The nightingale sings until dawn, the first dawn. And now we anticipate the second one. Now we expect the sign.

Endnotes

1. The original, Swedish version of this book was intended for use throughout the seven weeks of the Lenten season. Yet the theme of Lent—Christ's suffering and its significance for us who follow him—which is so eloquently expressed in this little book, ministers to us throughout the year. Those who wish to use the book's meditations as a Lenten guide are warmly encouraged to do so, but its message, as author Lena Malmgren puts it, is appropriate "for every other time when consolation is needed or when questions arise about suffering and about the meaning of life." If you would like to use this book as a Lenten reader, beginning with the second chapter you will find a meditation for each and every day of all seven weeks, from the Sunday before Lent (Quinquagesima) to the Saturday before Easter (Holy Saturday). The very first chapter, "Through Darkness into Light," includes meditations for the third and the second Sundays before Lent begins (the so-called Septuagesima and Sexagesima Sundays). One of the days in the fourth week is devoted to Mary's Annunciation.—Trans.

2. Gustaf Wingren (1911–2001) served as professor of theology and ethics at the University of Lund, 1951–1977; Ludvig Jönsson (1923–1985) was dean in Stockholm; Nathan Söderblom (1866–1931) served as archbishop of the Church of Sweden; American Harold Kushner is a Jewish rabbi.—Trans.

3. P. Nilsson (1906).

4. Stig Dagerman (1923–1954), gifted Swedish novelist, short-story writer, poet, and journalist, died by his own hand at thirty-one years of age.

5. Olof Hartman (1906–1982), pastor, theologian, author, and cultural critic, was one of Sweden's foremost twentieth-century preachers.

6. Nathanael Beskow (1865–1953), Swedish hymnist, educator, and preacher. The lines quoted here are from his 1919 hymn "Tränger i dolda djupen ner" ("My thoughts to secret depths may strive").

7. A hyrax is a small rodent-like creature found in rocky terrain of Asia and Africa, and mentioned here and there in Scripture, including Psalm 104:8. See also Leviticus 11:5; Proverbs 30:26.

8. The Nativity of St. John the Baptist is celebrated on June 24, which is also Sweden's Midsummer holiday.

9. Well-known hymn by Lina Sandell-Berg (1832–1903), who was equally famous for her hymn "Children of the Heavenly Father" and others.

10. Contemporary Swedish folk singer, born in Finland in 1944.

11. Inti-Illimani is a popular contemporary Chilean folk group. The song is by Swedish songwriter Violetta Parra (1917–1967), who lived and worked in Chile. The first line runs: "I want to thank life; it has given me so much."

12. Twentieth-century Swedish-Finnish novelist.

13. Sweden's southernmost province.

14. The word "cosmos" here is exactly the word used in the Greek original of John 3:16; it certainly refers to the world of humanity, but it also embraces creation in its fullness.

15. Published in Swedish in 1998, with the support of the Swedish Prime Minister Göran Persson, for a conference on the Holocaust. Its purpose was to begin from the Holocaust and "to take up questions of common humanity, democracy, and the equal worth of all human beings." The book was distributed without cost to any who requested it. The title comes from Joel 1:2–3.

16. A ferry between Estonia and Sweden, sunk in a storm on September 28, 1994. Around 900 drowned, and those who survived were almost without exception the young and healthy.

17. A scenic coastal site in north-central Sweden; childhood home of the author's husband and site of their summer house.—Trans.

18. A feature of Nordic folklore: female wood-sprites lured isolated wood cutters and charcoal makers deep into the forests and then abandoned them to their fates.

19. Fibromyalgia is now recognized by some experts as an autoimmune, non-inflammatory, rheumatic condition.

20. Although the English words to the same familiar hymn are slightly different, I've preserved the sense of the Swedish version because it serves the present context.—Trans.

21. Elsa Beskow (1874–1953), beloved Swedish author and illustrator of children's books.

22. Alice Tegnér (1864–1943), Swedish musician and composer of many children's songs.

23. This section was originally written for a worship service at the annual meeting of women pastors in the Swedish Church, Spring 2000.

24. Less dramatically perhaps, but no less lethally, Hanford and Three Mile Island.—Trans.

25. Birgitta Trotzig, b. 1929, Roman Catholic novelist and writer, and member of the Swedish Academy. Much of her work centers on themes of guilt and freedom.

26. Matthew 6:11. Various recent English translations retain the traditional "our daily bread," but observe in a marginal note that the rendering "our bread for tomorrow"—or something similar—is also possible.

27. The feast day in early February, celebrating the day Joseph and Mary brought the infant Jesus to the temple in Jerusalem for the rites of purification (Luke 2:22), that is, nearly a year after their "wedding."

28. The BBC's David Attenborough is responsible for half a century of informative and ecologically oriented programming on television and in film.

29. Rachel Carson's book *Silent Spring* (Houghton-Mifflin, 1962) was a ground-breaking treatment of the way humanity is destroying the environment.

30. Thor Heyerdahl (1914–2002), Norwegian marine biologist and explorer, sailed a primitive balsa-wood raft, the *Kon-Tiki*, across the Pacific Ocean in 1947.

31. In Greek mythology, Cronus was one of the Titans; he swallowed his own children at their birth to prevent them from overthrowing him.

32. One of Sweden's southwestern provinces, where the author grew up. The port city of Göteborg (Gothenburg) is its largest.

33. A region along the high bluffs forming the southeast shore of Vänern, the largest lake in Sweden.

34. The magnificent seventeenth-century castle at Läckö, all in white, sits on a point of land across a bay from the bluffs of Kinnekulle.

35. The province of Värmland borders Västergötland to the north, much of their boundary being formed by Lake Vänern.

36. The usual practice in previous centuries.

37. January 6 (in Sweden referred to as the Thirteenth Day of Christmas).

38. A small wooden, handheld frame, shaped something like an ancient lyre but smaller, and used for weaving bands of cloth. The author's own *bandgrind measures about 6½" x 9"*.

39. Hezekiah's amazing engineering feat, including the tunnel for conveying water into the city, can still be seen today; it remains one of Jerusalem's more popular tourist attractions.

40. Herbalists claim that figs contain certain antibacterial properties.

41. Opening line of one of the most frequently sung of Swedish hymns: "How glorious the earth! How glorious God's heaven! How beautiful our pilgrimage." It is set to the same tune as "Fairest Lord Jesus."

42. Title of a famous piece from Norwegian composer Edvard Grieg's suite of music (1876) for Henrik Ibsen's play *Peer Gynt*; Anitra, an alluring Egyptian dancer hoodwinks the foolish Peer Gynt out of his ill-got gains. The music for the dance is light, swirling, and Eastern.

43. Also from Grieg's *Peer Gynt* suite; the mountain troll king, in defense of his daughter, forces Peer Gynt to take responsibility for fathering her child. The music depicts the ominous thudding, tramp of trolls deep within the mountains, similar to Tolkien's later depiction of the treading of orcs in the mines of Moria

44. It is worth noting that this text from Luke 12:35 echoes the instructions to Israel regarding readiness for the exodus from Egypt (Exodus 12:11).

45. Evidently, the dike or dam must be built before the river's water level drops, in order to take advantage of snowmelt for operating a water-wheel-driven mill.

46. *Selenicereus grandiflorus,* a night-blooming cactus, native to Cuba; its enormous blossoms are pollinated by bats.